Come Inside

A Special Collection of Poetic Expressions
To help Move, Soothe, Lift, Encourage, and Inspire
To Comfort, to Console, to Teach, and to Reach
And to Lift the Name of the Most Holy Higher

Beverly Leonard
"The Poet with a Message"

Come Inside
© Beverly Leonard, 2006
All rights reserved

No part of this book may be used or reproduced in any manner without written permission of the author, except for brief quotation used in reviews and critiques.

Printed in the United States of America.

Published by WingSpan Press, Livermore, CA
www.wingspanpress.com

The WingSpan name, logo and colophon are the trademarks of WingSpan Publishing.

EAN 978-1-59594-074-2
ISBN 1-59594-074-X

First Edition 2006

Library of Congress Control Number. 2006931449

In precious memory of my beloved parents

Mr. Vance Murray Robertson, II
and
Mrs. Stella Rene Gipson-Robertson

Together again, at last!

DEDICATION

The words that have been caught and captured within
Have been written exclusively and is dedicated
To all of God's beautiful and beloved earthly children
May the nations feed and feast upon the words and become full
And may the humble Fisherwoman continue to be blessed
With the abilities to toss, capture, catch, seize, and pull

ACKNOWLEDGMENTS

First and foremost, I give thanks to the Lord on High
For, I prayed that He would send me "something" special
And He heard my meek, sincere, and heartfelt cry
He sent me the gifts of the written and spoken word
So, it is my obligation and duty these messages to spread
All honor, praise, and glory belong to the Lord on High
For, He is still on His heavenly and holy throne
He is still almighty, omnipotent, powerful, and strong
Thank you, oh, Lord, for the gifts
To my husband and to my three dear and precious children
Thank you for putting up with me through thick and through thin
I know the house got a lot messy and papers were everywhere
While I was busy capturing these thoughts with my paper and my pen
But you really didn't complain, and we all managed to stay sane
And, for this, I am truly grateful
Thank you, Floyd, Sr., Floyd, Jr., Ashley, and Alexa
To my siblings, my kin, and my friends at Frederick Douglass School
To my Pastor and First Lady, the Rev. and Mrs. C. W. Wallace
Thank you all for being there when I needed someone to listen to me
Whether face-to-face, by e-mail, or on the telephone
Thank you for your support and for encouraging me to ***"Write On"***
Thanks to each of you
To my dear aunt, Mrs. Imogene Edwards, who died in 1973
Who, when I was a little girl, saw something special and unique in me
For, without her guidance, her support, and her nurturing ways
Chances are, I probably would not be the person that I am today
Thank you, my sweet aunt, for being there for me
Last, but certainly not least, I thank you, the readers
For, without you, dear readers, my gifts would all be in vain
May something that is written within these pages
Touch you in positive and up-lifting ways
May you find hope, inspiration, comfort, and encouragement
May they touch your heart, mind, and soul, this I pray
Thank you, dear readers of these words

To everyone above, I extend a heart-felt thank you
Beverly Leonard, "The Poet with a Message"

TABLE OF CONTENTS

Chapter One
Beginnings
1

Chapter Two
Trials and Tribulations
31

Chapter Three
Words of Comfort and Encouragement
59

Chapter Four
Relationships: The Ins and the Outs
89

Chapter Five
Just Look to the Children
123

Chapter Six
Death and Dying: Not the Final Chapter
151

Chapter Seven
From the Depths of my Blackness
177

Chapter Eight
Praise the Lord
211

Chapter Nine
Last Words
241

A Special Tribute to Marvin Pentz Gaye, Jr.
The Man, His Message, and His Music
261

Come Inside

Come inside my inner room
The sanctuary of my mind
Please walk with me as I travel here and there
And thought provoking issues you will certainly find
Life, love, death, happiness, hope, and good cheer
Joy, pain, peace, comfort, and wisdom are all found here
And though we may not agree or see exactly eye to eye
One thing will certainly become quite crystal clear
Your mind will be provoked, enlightened, challenged, or stroked
If you take a walk inside here
Come Inside

Reflections of Life

Poetry reflects life
Like a giant mirror peering back at me
The good, the bad, the happy, and the sad
The joy, the pain, the hurt, and the misery
So, as I live, I capture these reflections of life
Through my God-given gift of sweet, sweet poetry
Reflections of Life

Chapter One
Beginnings

Give God the Glory

There are those who thrive on power, wealth, and fame
While seeking to bring honor and glory to their name
They walk around haughty with their heads in the clouds
For they are conceited, boisterous, vain, egotistical, and proud
Yet, we must be very careful how we view ourselves
For it may cause us, as well as others, to fall and stumble
Besides, God has ways of dealing with such haughty ones
Yes, God has ways of making us meek, mild, and humble
Remember the king by the name of Uzziah
Who was very successful just as long as he sought the good Lord
But his power went to his head, and eventually he was misled
So, God struck King Uzziah with leprosy upon his forehead
And remember Nebuchadnezzar, the mighty Babylonian king
And how, with himself, he too, became full
And because he failed to give God the glory
God took away his sanity, and for seven long years
King Nebuchadnezzar ate vegetation like a bull
And, in the end, this king had to accept and acknowledge
That God's glory should never be disregarded, ignored, or denied
For he experienced first-hand just how our Heavenly Father above
Is able to humiliate and bring shame to those walking in pride
Then there was Moses, who God chose to lead His people
Up and out of Egypt and into the Promise Land
But Moses, too, became full of himself
And upon the Promise Land, Moses was not allowed to stand
For, when God's people were thirsty out in the desert
With no watering hole in which to go
God instructed Moses to strike the rock
And from the rock the waters did indeed flow
But Moses failed to give the glory back to the Lord
And because he failed before the Israelites to lift God's holy name
The promise that God gave to His people, Moses was unable to claim
So, when we receive true blessings from the good Lord above
No matter what these blessings are
We must remember to give the glory back to the Lord
And the Lord shall continue to lift us up and carry us far
Give God the Glory

I Am Nothing

I am nothing without the love of the Lord
For my very existence depends totally upon Him
He who created the Heavens and the Earth
He who knew me before my earthly birth
I am nothing without the love of the Lord
I am nothing without the goodness of the Lord
For He provides me with all of my daily needs
In both good times and when times get hard
I am nothing without the goodness of the Lord
I am nothing without the kindness of the Lord
For He strengthens me when times get difficult and rock-hard
He lifts me up when life tries to knock me down
His Word is an anchor onto my feet
For it keeps me centered and on solid ground
I am nothing without the kindness of the Lord
I am nothing without the mercy and compassion of the Lord
For without God's mercy, His compassion, and His grace for Mankind
Mankind would have been destroyed long, long ago
But because the Lord loves and cares for us so
To Him for mercy and compassion we all can freely go
I am nothing without the mercy and compassion of the Lord
Oh, thank you, Heavenly Father
For your undying love sent down from Heaven above
Thank you for your goodness and for your kindness, too
Thank you for your mercy, your compassion, and for your saving grace
For there is no way I could ever make it without you
And thank you, Father, for your Word that you so lovingly left behind
So that true wisdom and the hope of salvation we all can find
Thank you, Heavenly Father, for without you, I am nothing
I Am Nothing

~ ~ ~

Welcome to my Soul

You have now entered the sanctuary of my soul
Through the words that you now behold
Welcome to my Soul

So Honored

I am so honored that God has found favor with me
And blessed me with the sweet, sweet gift of poetry
Like manna falling from Heaven above
Words filled with messages of hope, goodwill, wisdom, and love
Yes, I am so honored that God has found favor with me
And blessed me with the sweet, sweet gift of poetry
May the Lord continue to find favor with me
For I am so honored
So Honored

~ ~ ~

I've Got to Make a Difference

I've got to make a difference before I leave this old world
I've got to touch the heart, mind, and soul
Of some man, woman, boy, or girl
I've got to lift, love, encourage, and inspire
I've got to lift the Lord's holy and righteous name higher and higher
I've got to teach and reach God's earthly flock
And bring them closer to the One and Only True and Solid Rock
Yes, I've got to make a difference before I leave this old world
I've got to touch the heart, mind, and soul
Of some man, woman, boy, or girl
I've Got to Make a Difference

~ ~ ~

One Great Thing

If I could do one great thing to help Mankind
It would be to lead someone to Jesus Christ
So that they, too, can find salvation and eternal life
Yes, if I could do one great thing to help Mankind
It would be to lead someone to Jesus Christ
One Great Thing

What Kind of Person Would I Be

What kind of person would I be
If I fail to live according to God's holy will
For His holy will is that we love Him first and also one another
So, what kind of person would I be
If I fail to love God first and also my sisters and my brothers
What kind of mother would I be
If I fail to rear, raise, teach, and train my children well
For a mother's job is to love, nurture, and care her children
And help prevent their souls from burning in Hell
So, what kind of mother would I be
If I fail to teach, discipline, and train my children well
What kind of teacher would I be
If I fail to enrich the lives and the minds of my students
For a teacher's duty is to enlighten, lift, encourage, and inspire
To satisfy their natural thirst for learning
And to help keep their thirst for knowledge afire
So, what kind of teacher would I be
If I fail to enlighten, lift, encourage, and inspire
What kind of sister would I be
If I fail to help my siblings along life's way
For it is true, we are our brothers' keeper
No matter what the devil may think or say
So, what kind of sister would I be
If I fail to help my siblings along life's way
What kind of friend would I be
If I fail to be loyal, trustworthy, and true
For a true friend hangs tight to the very end
A true friend hangs tight through thick and through thin
So, what kind of friend would I be
If I fail to be a loyal, trustworthy, and true friend
What kind of Christian would I be
If I fail to help spread God's holy and inspired Word
For a Christian's obligation is to help save the souls of others
To help spread the Good News to our sisters and our brothers
So, what kind of Christian would I be
If I fail to help proclaim God's Kingdom to others
What Kind of Person Would I Be

Poetry Is Everywhere

Poetry can be found everywhere
In everything and in every situation
Poetry can be found in all of creation
From the early morning sunrise to the setting of the sun
Poetry can be found at all times
From late evening dusk to early morning dawn
On land and in the water and also in the air
Poetry can be seen, heard, and felt here, there, and everywhere
From the promise of a tiny seed to the giant and majestic sequoia tree
From the creepy crawly insects to the true giants of the seas
From the snow-capped mountains to the trenches beneath the seas
To the homes and habitats of the people
To the honeycombs of the bumblebees
From the hot and arid deserts to the cold and arctic lands
From the tranquil moments of quiet meditation
To the loud and boisterous noise of the enthusiastic sport fans
From the sounds of true laughter to the tears of the down-hearted
Poetry was even present when the Red Sea was parted
From the time of conception within a mother's womb
To the day of birth in the delivery room
Poetry abides within each of us
It even resides in the memorial tombs
And then beyond death and dying
To the melodic songs the angels sing
As they add music to their words
And lift their voices in praise to the holy King
Yes, poetry can be found everywhere
In everything and in every situation
From the center of the Earth
To the ends of the universe
Poetry can be found in all of creation
For poetry is everywhere
Poetry Is Everywhere

Come Inside   *Beverly Leonard*

The Gifts of Poets

If I were an *artist*, I would capture on canvas
Magnificent slices and scenes of life
Portraits of good times and happy times
Visions of sadness, suffering, sorrow, and strife
The beauty of the dawn and the setting of the sun
Raindrops dripping on an old country barn
Yes, if I were an artist, I'd capture on canvas these scenes of life
And I would present them each to you
If I were a *singer*, I would sing beautiful songs with soulful lyrics
And capture life's stories through ballads, oh, so sweet
I would even sing some of them down home blues
When life becomes a bit too heavy and tries to knock me off my feet
Yes, if I were a singer, I would sing beautiful songs with soulful lyrics
And I would serenade you with a song
If I were a *dancer*, the movements of my body
Would capture the depths of my every passion and emotion
And with the sway of my hips and my tilts and my dips
I would dance as if under the influence of a powerful potion
Yes, if I were a dancer, the movements of my body
Would capture the depths of my every passion and emotion
And I would dance a jig for you
If I were an *architect*, I would build you a kingdom both great and grand
It would be a kingdom so strong and fortified
That even through harsh and troubled times
Your kingdom would always and forever stand
Yes, if I were an architect, I would build you a great kingdom
And the keys to this kingdom I would place into your hands
Well, I paint with words and I sing with words
And with words I dance and build kingdoms both great and small
For the Lord has blessed me with the gift of the written word
To help uplift the human spirit when our spirits sometimes fall
So, here is your portrait and here is your song
Here is your dance and your kingdom, too
For, you will find all of these wonderful and enchanting gifts
Within the written words that I have captured just for you
For these are the gifts of poets
The Gifts of Poets

Waiting To Be Discovered

There exists in the midst of the masses and the madness
A poet waiting to be discovered by earthly man
Not just an ordinary poet, but a poet blessed with a special gift
To touch the minds and the hearts of the inhabitants of the land
And in her possessions are many inspired messages from Heaven above
Messages filled with hope, inspiration, wisdom, joy, and love
For this poet has been touched in an awesome and special way
To bring to the world these powerful and touching messages today
And like gentle doves, so full of hope, faith, and love
The messages are now ready to take wings and to the four corners fly
And of the Good News of God's Kingdom, they are ready to testify
For all must come to know of God's goodness, His mercy, and His grace
Before the world beholds His magnificent and glorious face
Yes, there exists in the midst of the masses and the madness
A poet waiting to be discovered by earthly man
But until it is God's holy will that this shall be
The humble poet shall continue to capture the thoughts
While waiting patiently
Waiting To Be Discovered

~ ~ ~

The Cherries on Top

Please don't let the word **"poetry"**
Prevent you from taking a walk with me
For the messages are real, they just happen to rhyme
Through my sweet, sweet gift of poetry
So, please don't let the word **"poetry"**
Cause your mind to prematurely stop
Besides, the rhyming words are simply the cherries on top
Now, come on inside and take a walk with me
Let us travel to higher levels of enlightenment
Through my God-given gift of poetry
The Cherries on Top

When the Holy Spirit Calls You

When the Holy Spirit calls you, you will know it
For there will be nowhere to run, flee, or hide
There will be no way to deny, disregard, or ignore it
Yes, when the Holy Spirit calls you, you will know it
Remember Jonah who was called by the Holy Spirit
To deliver a message to those who had gone astray
But Jonah had a different plan in mind
So, he decided to get into a boat and sail the opposite way
But God has ways of getting our attention
Yes, he has effective ways of bringing us back around
Whether it's time to reflect in the belly of a whale
Or causing a donkey to speak
God has ways of lifting us up and turning us around
By sometimes knocking us off our feet
So, when the Holy Spirit calls upon you
To do, act, or say whatever needs to be said or done
You must heed the call and act accordingly
For it is a call from the Most High and Holy One
Yes, when the Holy Spirit calls you, you will know it
And you must act accordingly and not ignore it
When the Holy Spirit calls you, you must show it
When The Holy Spirit Calls You

~ ~ ~

Fueled By Faith

My faith is my fuel that keeps me going strong
It keeps me firmly rooted and moving right along
And when my spirit sometimes gets tired, weary, and weak
I'm strengthened by God's Holy Word that lifts me to my feet
For my faith is my fuel that keeps me going strong
It keeps me firmly rooted and moving right along
Fueled By Faith

Speak, Oh, Spirit

Speak, oh, Spirit that dwells deep within me
That wields and yields a double-edged, powerful, and swift sword
Speak, oh, Spirit and purge the words right through me
Heavenly, holy, and inspired messages from the good Lord

Speak, oh, Spirit of the pain and the suffering of the Black man
The most oppressed and stressed ones in all the land
Speak, oh, Spirit to God's beautiful Black daughters and sons
Help lift, enlighten, and encourage them and help them to stand

Speak, oh, Spirit of the sins of this wicked old world
Sins that are rooted in bigotry, ignorance, temptation, and greed
Speak, oh, Spirit of the sins that devastate, doom, and destroy
Speak of these negative, deadly, and destructive seeds

Speak, oh, Spirit of the joy found only in the good Lord
For real happiness and peace of mind are found only in Him
Speak, oh, Spirit to the entire inhabited Earth
And help bring the masses of Mankind into the Lord's holy realm

Speak, oh, Spirit of the love that God has for all Mankind
For, another love like it in all the universe, we cannot find
Speak, oh, Spirit of His great agape love
That rains down blessings upon us from Heaven above

Speak, oh, Spirit of the hope that God has given to the world
To every man, woman, adolescent, boy, and girl
Speak, oh, Spirit of the hope of resurrection and everlasting life
When God shall put an end to sin, suffering, death, hell, and strife

Speak, oh, Spirit that dwells deep within me
That wields and yields a double-edged, powerful, and swift sword
Speak, oh, Spirit and purge the words right through me
Heavenly, holy, and inspired messages from the good Lord
Speak, Oh, Spirit

My Spirit Inside

My spirit inside is awakened, aroused, alert, and alive
Trying hard to maintain, hang, persevere, and survive
My spirit inside looks outside at the world and sadly sees
Great heartache, hurt, sorrow, pain, and misery
My spirit inside grieves, weeps, wails, and moans
To see all the sadness and suffering that's going on
My spirit inside is strengthened, reinforced, and fortified
By the blood of the One, who, for our sins on Calvary died
My spirit inside is trying to get back home
For, it knows that on this earthly plane it doesn't belong
My spirit inside longs to be set free
Free to reside forever beside the Lord in Paradise eternally
Yes, my spirit inside longs to be set free
At the end of my earthly journey
May the Lord continue to bless my spirit inside
And may my spirit inside in God's holy realm forever abide
May it love God first and also one another
For my spirit inside realizes that through His blood
We are all true sisters and brothers
All on an earthly journey trying to get back home
Where our spirits belong
My Spirit Inside

~ ~ ~

It's My Time to Fly

It's my time to fly said the gentle dove
It's my time to soar both far and wide
To do my part to help spread wisdom, hope, joy, and love
It's my time to fly said the gentle dove
It's My Time to Fly

The Poet Cometh

The poet cometh baring messages from on high
Blessed and highly favored by the good Lord above
To help spread peace, hope, wisdom, insight, and love
The Poet Cometh

~ ~ ~

Oh, Listen to the Words of the Poet

Oh, listen to the words of the poet
For the poet brings unto Mankind many wonderful things
So, listen with discernment to the words the poet brings
For the words of the poet are powerful, potent, and strong
They are deep, wide, extensive, broad, profound, and long
They comfort and console and they touch the human soul
They up-lift the down-hearted and strengthen the weak
They clarify and explain as well as educate and teach
And unto all Mankind they extend and they reach
The words of the poet motivate, encourage, and inspire
They help elevate and enhance Mankind higher and higher
For there is Spirit in the inspired words of the poet
Spirit which flows down from Heaven above
To help spread peace, joy, inspiration, wisdom, hope, and love
Spirit that flows from on high down to the mind of the poet
Then from the mind of the poet straight to you
To help you, my beloved ones, to make it on through
So, listen to the words of the poet
As the poet delivers the messages from on high to you
Oh, Listen to the Words of the Poet

~ ~ ~

As I Learn

As I learn I must teach
For Mankind's mind, heart, and soul I must somehow reach
To deliver holy and inspired messages from Heaven above
Messages from on high filled with hope, joy, peace, and love
As I Learn

Get In Where You Fit In

When I write, it is as if God Himself speaks directly to me
Inspired messages sent down from Heaven above
Teaching me, leading me, guiding me, and inspiring me
Holy messages of hope, faith, encouragement, life, and love
Sometimes the words stare back at me
For, they are messages to and for me as well
And I must often recall these words that are written
To help prevent my soul from burning in the flames of hell
They lift me up, strengthen, fortify, and console me
When I feel overwhelmed, stressed out, and burdened down
They comfort, encourage, and inspire me
And help keep my feet on solid ground
So, I capture these holy and inspired messages
With the power of the paper and the pen
Not only for myself, but for others as well
So, concerning my poetry
Get in where you fit in
Get In Where You Fit In

~ ~ ~

Not Mine But Thine

Sometimes I read the words that are recorded
And I am amazed and awed at the words myself
And I joyfully proclaim that the words are good
As if the words came from someone else
And as I step back and look at the big picture
I clearly see that the words don't really come from me
In other words, the words are not really mine
For I am merely a vessel being used by the Lord
To bring these messages to all Mankind
Oh, Lord, they are not mine, but thine
Not Mine But Thine

Perfect Calls

And God called out unto **Moses** to lead his people
Up and out of Egypt and into the Promise Land
Yes, God called Moses out from among the masses
To free his people from Pharaoh's hard, harsh, and heavy hand
And God called out unto **Jonah** to deliver a warning to a people
To a people who were living not according to God's holy will
And Jonah found out first hand while inside the belly of a whale
That it's best the Lord's holy will to carry out and fulfill
And God called out unto **John the Baptist**
To prepare the way for His only begotten and beloved Son
Yes, God called John the Baptist out to spread the Good News
Of the coming and of the glory of this holy and blessed one
And God called out unto **His only begotten Son**
To save from sin and from satan the lives of everyone
Yes, God called His only begotten Son out to draw all men unto Him
To draw all men unto His Father's most holy and perfect realm
And God called out unto **Martin** to help spread peace and goodwill
To speak out against injustices, inequalities, and other terrible ills
Yes, God called Martin out to speak out against bigotry and greed
By planting positive, up-lifting, and non-violent seeds
And God called out unto **Malcolm** to learn a better way
A way in which the nations of Allah could come together as one
Yes, God called Malcolm out and gave him true enlightenment
God showed him that unity as a people under God can be done
And God called out unto **Me** to deliver through my gift of poetry
Inspired and heavenly messages sent down from Heaven above
Messages that touch, teach, enlighten, inspire, and reach
Messages filled with hope, compassion, truth, wisdom, and love
Yes, God makes perfect calls and He's calling out to **You**
For there is something quite special the Lord wants you to do
Will you heed His call, or like Jonah, will you first have to fall
In order to rise to the occasion and carry out His holy call
And for those who fell or shall fall while lifting God's holy name
Everlasting life these hearers and doers of His Word shall claim
When the Giver, the Receiver, and the Restorer of life
Shall once again call their names
For the Lord makes perfect calls
Perfect Calls

The Fisherwoman

The Fisherwoman sits quietly with her paper and her pin
Hoping to capture and catch the thoughts that flow deep within
For many thoughts and ideas, like fish, swim around
Gliding in and out, this way and that way, up and down
A large one swims to the surface top and nibbles at her mind
One with great power and potential to help feed Mankind
And the good Lord who looks down upon her from Heaven above
Blesses her with the power of the paper and the pen
Yes, the Lord blesses the humble Fisherwoman
To be a blessing to earthly men
So, into the sea of thoughts the Fisherwoman tosses her pole
In search of powerful words that can touch the human soul
She searches for words that will lift, encourage, and inspire
Words that will enhance and elevate Mankind higher and higher
And soon with great determination and with the help of the Lord
The Fisherwoman captures and catches the thought
And the words that will help heal the nations
Are now hooked, snared, seized, and caught
May the nations feed upon the words and become full
And may the humble Fisherwoman continue to be blessed
With the abilities to wait, toss, capture, catch, and pull
The Fisherwoman

~ ~ ~

Sometimes I Can Just Stand Back

Sometimes I can just stand back and clearly see
Just what the Lord has done and is still doing for me
I can feel His Holy Spirit as it connects with mine
I can sense His holy presence that is omnipotent and divine
Yes, sometimes I can just stand back and clearly see
Just what the Lord has done and is still doing for me
Sometimes I Can Just Stand Back

I'm Just a Messenger

I'm just a messenger with a message of love
A message of love sent down from Heaven above
I'm just a messenger with a message of love
I'm just a messenger with a message of hope
Hope for God's people that will help His people to cope
I'm just a messenger with a message of hope
I'm just a messenger with a message of peace
Let's stop the madness now and let the violence cease
I'm just a messenger with a message of peace
I'm just a messenger with a message of joy
For the Lord has promised everlasting life
And death and dying He shall soon destroy
I'm just a messenger with a message of joy
And these messages of love, hope, peace, and joy
I deliver unto you to help you make it through
I'm Just a Messenger

~ ~ ~

I'm a Poet

I'm a poet and I know it
For the Lord has blessed me with the awesome gift of poetry
Yes, I'm a poet and I know it, but please don't think I'm vain
For all the praise and glory belong to the One who gave it to me
And through my gift, I shall forever lift the Lord's holy name
I'm a Poet

~ ~ ~

It's Not About Me

It's not about me, the messenger
But it's all about the messages that are found within
Moreover, it's all about the One who gave them to me
To deliver to Mankind through my God-given gift of poetry
It's Not About Me

The Messages Within the Poetry

As you peruse these lines that flow and rhyme
Make sure the messages within the poetry you find
For the messages are real, they just happen to rhyme
So, make sure the messages within the poetry you find
The Messages Within the Poetry

~ ~ ~

Through Poetry

Through poetry, I tiptoe, I run, I leap, I bound, and I jump
Through poetry, I slip, I slide, I swagger, I fall, and go **BUMP**
Through poetry, I whisper softly, I sing, I dance, I chant, and I shout
Through poetry, I ponder, I wonder, and I figure things out
Through poetry, I giggle, I grin, I laugh, and I smile
Through poetry, I trek, I trudge, I tread, and I walk those extra miles
Through poetry, I weep, I wail, I whine, and sometimes I moan
Through poetry, I'm comforted and consoled when I'm sad and alone
Through poetry, I teach and through poetry I reach
Through poetry, I've been known to sometimes preach
Through poetry, I lift and praise God's holy and righteous name
Through poetry, His omnipotence and glory I proudly proclaim
Through poetry, I am blessed by the good Lord above
Through poetry, I plant seeds of hope, wisdom, joy, and love
Through poetry, I touch the minds and the hearts of Mankind
Through poetry, I purge my soul and find joy and peace of mind
Through poetry, I endure great heartaches and strife
Through poetry, I celebrate and venerate the gift of life
Through poetry, I can face death and dying and not fear
Through poetry, I know that God is always and forever near
Through poetry, may I continue to be highly blessed
To be a blessing to my fellow man
To encourage and inspire and to lend a helping hand
Through poetry may I continue along life's way
Until my earthly journey is over, said, and done
And then through poetry may my spirit reside forever
In the presence of the most holy One
Through Poetry

In Poetry and in Life

Just as in life sometimes
I'll get lost in a poem and lose my way
So many thoughts being captured, seized, and caught
That I sometimes forget what I was originally trying to say
And in times like these I must stop and go back
And find out just when, where, why, and how my mind got off track
Just as I do in life when I sometimes lose my way
I have to stop and think back
And find out just when, where, why, and how my life got off track
In Poetry and in Life

~ ~ ~

A Poet's Panic

A poet panics when thoughts are flowing
And the poet cannot find a pencil or a pen
To capture the thoughts that flow deep within
Yes, such are the times when panic in a poet sets in
A Poet's Panic

~ ~ ~

Purple Crayon

I could not find a pencil nor could I find a pen
To capture the thoughts that were flowing deep, deep within
And soon, apprehension, panic, and alarm set in
For such is the scenario when a poet cannot find a pen
So, I searched and I searched and I searched some more
For this important task surely had to be done
And eventually after a feverish and frantic search
The good Lord blessed me to find a purple crayon
Purple Crayon

I Write Accordingly

I write according to how life
Moves me
Soothes me
Pushes me
Pulls me
Pinches me
Punches me
Touches me
Nudges me
Strokes me
Pokes me
Provokes me
Comforts me
Consoles me
Cuddles me
Molds me
Loves me
Impresses me
Caresses me
Oppresses me
Rubs me
Hugs me
Slaps me
Enwraps me
Tempts me
Trips me
Entraps me
Teaches me
Chastises me
Tries me
Bumps me
Thumps me
Scolds me
Pushes me
Picks me up
And tenderly holds me
I write accordingly
I Write Accordingly

When the Poet Cries

When the poet cries while writing the lines that rhyme
The poet is purging the hurt and the pain the poet feels inside
But not to worry, for the poet will be just fine
When the poet cries while writing the lines that rhyme
And you can be sure that the words which caused the poet to cry
Will touch many hearts, minds, and souls bye and bye
When the Poet Cries

~ ~ ~

The Room

Dark, empty, cold, and barren is the room inside
Before the poets come with their spoken words
That will cause the room to awaken and come alive
Yes, the spoken words of the poets will give life to the room
Like a baby bouncing with joy inside its mother's womb
Nurtured by the words that flow all around
For, in the words of the poets, many nutrients are found
Like the Breath of Life that God blew into Mankind
When He created man from the cool, cool ground
But all too soon, the poets shall leave and depart from the room
And once again, the room shall become
Like a dark, empty, cold, and barren womb
Until the next time the poets come and give life to the room
The Room

~ ~ ~

It Was a Poet

It was a poet who penned the words of that song
You know that song that you love the very best
The one that grabs your mind, heart, and soul
The one that touches your spirit more than the rest
Yes, it was a poet who penned the words of that song
That song that you love the very best
May the poets of the world continue to be blessed
It Was a Poet

The Party

The thinkers came to the party that day
And so did the poets, the musicians, and the singers, too
The dancers showed up wearing their dancing shoes
And the artists were there with their artsy crew
First, the thoughts began flowing from the thinkers' minds
Then the poets captured the thoughts and made them all rhyme
The musicians then took the rhymes and added some real cool beats
Then the singers sang out and the dancers got upon their feet
Oh, what a good time they all had that day
As they thought, rhymed, jammed, sang, and danced the night away
And the artists who were also gifted, creative, imaginative, and keen
Captured on canvas the entire joyful and jovial scene
And they partied hearty throughout the course of the night
Well into the wee and early morning light
Until the thinkers had to rest their tired and weary minds
And the poets could no longer dish out the rhymes
The musicians stopped playing their harmonies
The singers stopped singing their melodies
The dancers stopped dancing and prancing around
And the artists' paintbrushes fell to the ground
Then they all went their separate ways
After saying their good-byes and all
Now, the only remnant that remains of the party
Is the painting that still hangs on the wall
The Party

~ ~ ~

My Calling

Teaching is my calling
To help enlighten and elevate the Human mind
And to help lift those who are falling
Yes, teaching is my calling
My Calling

Simply Divine

I prayed for divine knowledge and divine knowledge came my way
I prayed for divine wisdom and divine wisdom came, too
I prayed for divine understanding
And divine understanding came on through
So, there stood my three divines
My divine **knowledge**, **wisdom**, and **understanding**
But with them all what was I now to do
Soon true enlightenment came my way
And I discovered that what was missing was divine **discernment**
The ability to know how, when, where
And with whom to share my divines with
Well, I still pray for divine knowledge, wisdom, and understanding
But now I pray for divine discernment, too
For when all of my divine divines are divinely combined
My divinely combined divines divinely carry me through
Simply Divine

~ ~ ~

With This Mind

With this mind I can brainstorm, produce, invent, and beget
With this mind I can concoct, conceive, construct, and connect
With this mind I can formulate, motivate, and collaborate
With this mind I can devise, design, plan, and create
With this mind I can build, construct, and generate
With this mind I can touch, teach, train, and reach
With this same mind I can exterminate, eradicate, and eliminate
With this same mind I can annihilate, obliterate, and devastate
With this same mind I can plunder, abolish, demolish, and terminate
With this same mind, I can create chaos, conflict, and confusion
With this same mind, I can wreck, ruin, ravage, and cause disillusion
Yes, with this mind, I can do both good and bad, and so can you
But let us do that which is good, honest, uplifting, kind, and true
Let us do these things to strengthen and enhance Mankind
So that peace, progress, and prosperity we all shall find
With This Mind

This Thing I Do

This thing I do is nothing new
For poets have been penning their thoughts since the world first began
In fact, poets have been purging and splurging on words and rhyme
Even before the creation of the Earth and earthly man
For, you see, long before the Earth and Mankind were created
The angels joyfully sang out all around God's holy throne
Words penned and recorded by God's heavenly hosts
Who then added music and turned their poetic words into song
So, you see, this thing I do is nothing new
And as long as there is life, and even beyond death and dying
There will always be poets purging their hearts and minds
For this thing I do is nothing new
This Thing I Do

~ ~ ~

First, Second, and Third Person Poems

First person poems are all about me
They are to me, for me, and straight up at me
And if you think you really, really know me
You'll recognize me in my first person poetry
Because first person poems are all about me
Second person poems are all about you
Whomever you may happen to be
They are talking to you, about you, and straight up at you
You'll quickly claim them when you read or hear them
Because second person poems are all about you exclusively
Third person poems are all about life
The ups, the downs, the ins, and the outs
The joys, the pains, the happiness, and the strife
Because third person poems are all about life
First, Second, and Third Person Poems

Whose Shoes

True poets write from their hearts
Oftentimes exposing who they really are deep, deep inside
Taking you deep and deeper into the depths of their inner minds
Until nothing but raw reality you do indeed find
True poets are also blessed with the unique ability
To mentally and emotionally walk in someone else's shoes
And feel the feelings they're feeling deep inside
Whether it's love overflowing or some of them down home blues
So, when you come inside my inner mind
You may find yourself asking, "Whose shoes"
Well, only the poets and the good Lord know for sure
And maybe a few – maybe one or two
But then maybe not
Whose Shoes

~ ~ ~

The Artist and the Poet

The artist and the poet went to the Master one day
And together they asked the Master
Master, who is greater - the artist or the poet
Is it the artist who captures on canvas
Scenes of happiness, joy, sadness, and strife
Or is it the poet who purges through words
Words that reflect the same conditions of life
Who is greater – the artist or the poet
And the Master answered
Neither is greater than the other
For the artist paints visual images
And from these visual images
Thoughts and ideas in the mind are formed
Whereas, the poet uses thoughts and ideas
And from these thoughts and ideas
Mental images in the mind are born
Neither is greater than the other
The Artist and the Poet

Sometimes I've Got to Get Away

Sometimes I've got to get away
From all the hustle and the bustle
That come with each and every passing day
Away from the problems, the pressures, and all of the strife
That comes with living, learning, loving, and life
Yes, I've got to get away sometimes
To help free my sometimes cluttered and chaotic mind
Away from the heartache, the hurt, and also the hell
That sometimes I know first hand and, oh, so well
Away from the worry, the stress, and the strain
Away from toxic, negative, and stinky thinking people
Who act crazy, stupid, silly, uncaring, and insane
Away from the children
Away from the house
Away from the noise
Away from my spouse
Away from my job
Away from the chores
Away from ringing phones and faxes
Away from loud and banging doors
Yes, sometimes I need to get away
But there is one thing that I can never get away from
And that is from the presence of the good Lord
For He was present even when I was in my mother's womb
And He will be there at the memorial tomb
Even after death and dying together we shall be
Together forever in Paradise eternally
But until the arrival of that great day
Sometimes I've got to get away
Sometimes I've Got to Get Away

~ ~ ~

Come and Go With Me

Come and go with me to a place where our minds can be free
Free as the birds that soar and ascend over land and sea
Yes, come and go with me to a place where our minds can be free
Come and Go With Me

To The Pond

To the pond I often go
To let my thoughts, my feelings, and my emotions flow
A quiet place to think things through
To meditate, to reflect, to read, and to write poetry, too
To enjoy the beauty of nature – the birds and the bees
The flowers, the ducks, and the beautiful trees
As well as the soothing water and the gentle breeze
Yes, sometimes to the pond I often go
To let my thoughts, my feelings, and my emotions flow
To The Pond

~ ~ ~

By The Pond

Sometimes I like to go and sit alone by the pond
To get away from everything and from everyone
To relax and unwind and free my often cluttered mind
For, by the pond, true peace of mind I can always find
The soft and soothing ripples of the waves call out unto me
So do the tall green grass, the flowers, and also the trees
The birds chirp and the creepy crawly insects crawl all about
And unto me, all of nature seems to shout and call out
The blue sky overhead and the soft clouds they hold
As well as the gentle breezes that refresh and ease my soul
They all seem to joyfully call out unto me
Proudly proclaiming God's goodness, His glory, and His majesty
Yes, sometimes I like to go and sit alone by the pond
And get away from everything and from everyone
To relax and unwind and free my often cluttered mind
For, by the pond, true peace of mind I can always find
By The Pond

God's Beautiful Garden

I love to visit God's beautiful garden
For sometimes He allows me to come right on in
And when I visit His beautiful garden
I always carry with me my paper and my pen
For, while we visit together in the splendor of His garden
We walk and we talk together along the way
And He tells me things He wants the world to know
So, I record the words and into the world the words will go
And once our visit comes to an end
I can hardly wait until I visit His beautiful garden once again
To experience the unspeakable peace and joy that is found within
And to record the inspired words to be delivered to earthly men
Yes, I love to visit God's beautiful garden
And I can't wait to go there again
God's Beautiful Garden

~ ~ ~

I'm Loving It

I'm loving the coolness of the wind
I'm loving the warmth of the sunshine upon my skin
I'm loving the ripples and the soft waves upon the pond
I'm loving the fountain as it spews, spurts, sprouts, and hums
I'm loving the blue sky and the green grass and tall tress
I'm loving the chirping of the birds and the buzzing of the bees
I'm loving the joggers and the walkers as they pass me by
I'm loving the peace of mind that I feel deep, deep inside
I'm loving the opportunity to be in the presence of the Most Holy
I'm loving nature, for it speaks of God's goodness and of His glory
I'm loving the time that I have to go deep inside of me
I'm loving sitting on the bench writing sweet, sweet poetry
I'm Loving It

Good Day Bugs

I invade their space in the early morning dawn
Before they creep, crawl, fly, and slither along
On the bench I sit with my paper and my pen
To capture the thoughts that flow deep within
In the presence of the Lord, I'm inspired to write
Messages of joy, hope, peace, pain, sorrow, and strife
Until the inhabitants of my borrowed space awaken
And notice that a stranger has entered within
And soon all of nature seems to come alive
Which causes me to close my pad and cap my pen
Good day spiders and good day mosquitoes
Good day bugs and insects known and unknown
For now, you have awakened to begin your day
And I've got to now move on
Good Day Bugs

~ ~ ~

Talking To Myself

There are some who say that talking to yourself
Is really a crazy and an insane thing to do
But I beg to differ on this statement made
For this statement is not entirely in itself true
For I talk to myself quite often these days
In the presence of the good Lord
And I talk myself into some rather deep and heavy thoughts
Thoughts that help me make it through in good times and hard
Now, I consider myself a pretty good conversationalist
So, why not talk and converse with myself
For by doing so, many things I have come to realize and know
So, if by chance you happen to see me talking to myself
And you don't see anyone else around
Please don't think that I've lost my mind
For it is my mind that I'm trying to find
Talking To Myself

In Solitude but Never Alone

Sometimes I sit in solitude with my paper and my pen
But I never sit completely alone
For I am always in the holy presence of the good Lord
And in one way or another, He makes his holy presence known
And many times I am completely awed by the words
At how they flow like honey from above with ease
And the thoughts behind the words are sometimes so powerful
They sometimes literally knock me to my knees
And sometimes the Lord has my rhyming words
Patiently waiting for me to get to the end
Then there are times when it rhymes without my knowledge
For the Lord is quicker than my human mind, paper, hand, and pen
And if by chance you happen to hear me say
That my poems are really, really good
Please know that I'm not trying to bring honor to myself
But I'm lifting the Lord's name instead
For it is He who gives me the thoughts and the words
Yes, sometimes I sit in solitude with my paper and my pen
But I never sit completely alone
For I am always in the presence of the good Lord
And in one way or another, He makes his holy presence known
In Solitude but Never Alone

~ ~ ~

Not the Mistakes, but the Messages

If, within the messages, spelling errors you find
While perusing the lines that flow and rhyme
Please know that the errors I diligently tried to find
Since I couldn't afford a professional proofreader at this time
And it's really quite hard my own mistakes to clearly see
So, if you find a few mistakes here and there, please, oh, please forgive me
Besides, it's not about the mistakes, but it's all about the messages
The messages that are found within the poetry
Not the Mistakes, but the Messages

The Fall of Man

So the Lord said to the Serpent:
"Because you have done this, you are cursed more than all cattle, and more than every beast of the field. On your belly you shall go, and you shall eat dust all the days of your life. And I will put enmity between you and the woman, and between your seed and her seed. He shall bruise your head and you shall bruise his heel."

To the Woman He said:
"I will greatly multiply your sorrow and your conception. In pain, you shall bring forth children. Your desire shall be for your husband, and he shall rule over you."

To the Man He said:
"Because you have heeded the voice of your wife, and have eaten from the tree of which I commanded you, saying, "You shall not eat of it". : Cursed is the ground for your sake; in toil you shall eat of it all the days of your life. Both thorns and thistles it shall bring forth for you, and you shall eat the herb of the field. In the sweat of your face, you shall eat bread till you return to the ground, for out of it you were taken; for dust you are, and to dust you shall return."

Genesis 3: 14-19

Chapter Two
Trials and Tribulations

Oh, Listen to the Earth

Oh, listen to the Earth
For the Earth is moaning and groaning
Can you hear her sounds of sorrow, sadness, and despair
For troubles, trials, and tribulations
Are running rampant upon the Earth everywhere
Oh, listen to the Earth
For the Earth is weeping and a' wailing
Can you see her tears flowing like the ancient River Nile
Crying for her children who are oppressed and weighed down
For true love for God and for one another can scarcely be found
Oh, listen to the Earth
For the Earth is aching and is experiencing excruciating pains
Can you feel her agony that runs long, wide, and deep
Making it difficult for society to stand firmly upon its feet
Causing humanity to collapse and crumble in one huge heap
But He who created the Heavens and also the Earth
And also the vastness of the massive universe
Says, **"Oh, listen to Me"**
"For even though the Earth
Is moaning and groaning
Weeping and a' wailing
Aching and experiencing excruciating pain and agony
I shall soon free her from her suffering, oppression, and misery"
Yes, soon the Earth shall suffer no more
For the Lord shall restore it to perfection as it was once before
He shall bring an end to death, dying, suffering, and sorrow
For He is still Alpha and Omega, the Beginning and the End
He is still the world's only hope for a brighter tomorrow
But until the Lord returns to set matters straight
Unfortunately for the inhabitants of the Earth
The Earth shall continue to decline, decay, and degenerate
Oh, listen to the Earth
For the Earth is moaning, groaning, weeping, wailing, and aching
Can you hear, see, and feel her terrible pains
Oh, Listen to the Earth

Come Inside   *Beverly Leonard*

The Days of Noah

The days of Noah are the days of today
For people are living their lives in the same old sinful ways
A world full of people doing things that are bad
Bringing displeasure and dishonor to the Lord and making him sad
Yes, the days of Noah are the days of today
People living their lives in the same old sinful ways
Parents not parenting and kids hitting the skids
Children lacking great shame, honor, morals, and respect
But when you look at the trees from whence they fell
And the world in which they live, what more should we expect
It's parents against their children
And children against their parents
White against Black against Brown against Red
Family against family and nation against nation
Instead of loving one another, we hate one another instead
And it's been like this ever since that ill-fated day
When Cain, who, in a jealous rage, his brother Abel he did slay
Yes, it was death in the first family on that dreadful day
And ever since then, it's been nothing but hell and heartache to pay
For from the Earth true peace and joy went away
And now it's just as bad, just as mad, and just as sad as it was before
For the acts of Mankind are putrid and bitter to the very core
It reminds me also of the days of Sodom and Gomorra
For people are behaving like they did back then
Before brimstone and fire from Heaven to the Earth did descend
But the Good News is that, like the days of Noah
And the days of Sodom and Gomorra, there will be survivors
Those who shall make it safely on through
Who, like Noah and Lot, there shall be those found who are true
And for these righteous ones, the Lord will make the Earth anew
But until that time comes
The days of Noah are the days of today
For people are living their lives in the same old sinful ways
Bent and steeped in sin are the hearts and mindsets of earthly men
Yes, the days of Noah are the days of today
The Days of Noah

The Hands of satan

satan has his hands in all of the activities of earthly man
We have only to look around and sorrowfully see
How his influence, power, domination, and control
Have caused and still cause Mankind nothing but misery
He viciously attacks the family structure
Assaulting the very foundation of the family and home
For it is his ultimate wish and desperate desire
To make all family members his very own

He can be found in the church and is always on the lurch
To attack those who are trying to be true and good
He is ever-present in the schoolhouse
The courthouse and even in the White House
For he is the original manslayer and manipulator
He is the original rogue, scoundrel, louse, and mischief-maker
He can clearly be seen and felt in the field of entertainment
On TV, on the radio, in technology, and on film
His ways are made manifest through shameful and sinful acts
Through dirty deeds that personify and glorify him

He is powerful in the boardroom and also in the bedroom
He is behind every war that has ever been fought
Whether it be in the mind, on land, in the water, and in the air
In fact, wherever chaos, corruption, and destruction are found
You can be assured that satan is present and right there
He plants and nurtures negative and bitter seeds
Seeds of bigotry, hatred, selfishness, disunity, and greed
He enters through the doorways of alcohol and drugs
That turn its victims into sad, mindless, and dangerous thugs

Yes, satan has his hands in all of the activities of earthly man
We have only to look around and sorrowfully see
How his influence, power, domination, and control
Have caused and still cause Mankind nothing but misery
So, be aware and beware of the hands of satan
The Hands of satan

Come Inside *Beverly Leonard*

Nobody but the devil

Who tempts and taunts us when our spirits are weary and weak
Nobody but the devil
Who tries everything by any means to knock us off our feet
Nobody but the devil
Who causes chaos, confusion, conflict, trouble, and strife
Nobody but the devil
Who wishes to destroy Mankind's hope for everlasting life
Nobody but the devil
Who wants us to be discouraged, sad, downhearted, and depressed
Nobody but the devil
Who enjoys seeing us overwhelmed, worried, burdened, and stressed
Nobody but the devil
Who causes contentions, divisions, envy, jealousy, and distrust
Nobody but the devil
Who uses every evil and deceptive trick to trap and ensnare us
Nobody but the devil
Who plots, plans, manipulates, hates, and misleads
Nobody but the devil
Who lies, betrays, schemes, seduces, lures, and deceives
Nobody but the devil
Who destroys friendships, kinships, and strong family bonds
Nobody but the devil
Who tries to steal the joy and peace of mind of everyone
Nobody but the devil
Who's behind all of life's suffering, sadness, pains, and sorrows
Nobody but the devil
Who fills Mankind with fear, terror, dread, and horror
Nobody but the devil
Who hates and despises the Father and his only begotten Son
Nobody but the devil
Who's angry because his time is almost over, said, and done
Nobody but the devil
Who will be thrown into the fiery bind
Nobody but the devil
Along with his evil demons and wicked Mankind
Nobody but the devil
Nobody but the devil

Fighting the devil

Fighting the devil is a very hard and difficult thing to do
For this manslayer is powerful, mighty, mean, and strong
And it is his ultimate desire and goal to destroy our very souls
By tempting us in our moments of weakness to err and do wrong
He assesses our weaknesses and sets his traps all around
Testing and enticing our hearts, minds, and souls
Hoping to knock us flat upon the cold, hard ground
When this evil one was kicked to the Earth from Heaven above
The angels sang out and rejoiced, but said, " Woe unto all Mankind"
For they knew the troubles, the trials, and the tribulations
That all Mankind would have, and still to this day
Troubles, trials, and tribulations have not gone away
And because this evil one knows that his time is nearly done
He's trying his very best to ensnare the souls of everyone
And because he knows firsthand just how his end shall end
He's angry and upset because he knows that into the hell fires
He and his deceptive demons shall soon descend
But until that day comes, satan will be working overtime
Scheming, plotting, planning, and manipulating
How to bring destruction to all Mankind
For, in this hater, love and compassion you cannot find
Yes, fighting the devil is a very hard and difficult thing to do
Hard, yes, difficult, yes, but impossible, no way
For there is a more powerful and omnipotent one
I speak of God the Father and with Him is His only begotten Son
The One, who, just the mention of His holy name
Causes satan and his demons to tremble and shake
For they know that He is almighty, all powerful, and great
And because this is a spiritual fight to destroy our souls
We need a strong spiritual leader who will help us
One who has not forgotten that we came from dust
One who still loves and cares so very much about us
Yes, fighting the devil is difficult, burdensome, and hard
But it is possible with the help of the good Lord
So, don't let satan steal your mind, your spirit, and your soul
But onto the good Lord quickly grab a strong hold
Fighting the devil

In Picking Times

When the bills are high and the money is low
We're ripe for picking
When we don't know which way to turn or which way to go
We're ripe for picking
When those we love the most fail to love us back
We're ripe for picking
When self-esteem, confidence, self-respect, and pride we lack
We're ripe for picking
When we stray away from the realm and the Word of the Lord
We're ripe for picking
When our lives and our living becomes extra difficult and hard
We're ripe for picking
When our houses are no longer loving homes
We're ripe for picking
When our hearts ramble, wonder, rove, rant, and roam
We're ripe for picking
When we don't have a family or a home to call our very own
We're ripe for picking
When we are tempted into sin by the desires of our hearts
We're ripe for picking
When our hearts are shattered, splattered, ripped, and torn apart
We're ripe for picking
When others talk about us behind our backs
We're ripe for picking
When our name and our integrity are both under attack
We're ripe for picking
When our spirits are tired, weary, worn, and weak
We're ripe for picking
When it's hard to stand steadfast and firm on our own two feet
We're ripe for picking
When our bodies ache and throb and are in great pain
We're ripe for picking
When the trials of life threaten to drive us completely insane
We're ripe for picking
When we are mistreated, neglected, hated, and rejected
We're ripe for picking
When we are insulted, dishonored, and disrespected

We're ripe for picking
When we are used, misused, taken for granted, and abused
We're ripe for picking
When we're unhappy, lonely, depressed, stressed, and blue
We're ripe for picking
When nothing seems to be going right for me and for you
We're ripe for picking
When we just don't know what to do
We're ripe for picking
When we fall victim to dangerous and mind-altering drugs
We're ripe for picking
When death claims the lives of those we love
We're ripe for picking
When blessings don't seem to flow upon us from Heaven above
We're ripe for picking
So, just what are we to do in times like these
When satan is doing all that he can to knock us to our knees
What are we to do in ripe times like these
When peace and joy cannot be found
But only heartache and sorrow in abundance abound
What do we do in times like these
Do we curse God and die
Do we ask Him over and over, "Why, oh, Lord, why"
Do we mope and pine in our sadness and a river of tears cry
Do we give up, out, and in and no longer attempt to even try
Or do we, like Job, hold on to our faith and keep our integrity
Do we endure until the end through all of our pain and misery
What do we do in times like these when we're ripe for picking
The choice is yours and the choice is mine
As to what we shall do in picking times
In Picking Times

~ ~ ~

So Hard

Sometimes life can be so hard
It makes you want to shout, "Oh, my Lord, why, oh, why so hard"
So Hard

Harder Than It Has To Be

Life in general is hard and heavy
Filled with great sadness, sorrow, and misery
But sometimes we make our lives much harder
Much harder than it has to be
For the decisions we make and the actions we take
Directly affect the consequences that we must face
And many times we end up hurting ourselves and others as well
And so much energy, time, and tears we unnecessarily waste
We must stop and realize just what we are doing with our lives
Before we lose everything we have achieved so far in life
For one day we may wake up and it will all be gone
And we'll be broken down, miserable, sad, and so all alone
Yes, life in general is hard and heavy
Filled with great sadness, sorrow, and misery
But sometimes we make our lives much harder
Much harder than it has to be
Let us not wait until it's too late
For we will be unable to turn back the hands of time
Let us think long and hard about the decisions we make
Or devastation and destruction will be our only fate
Harder Than It Has To Be

~ ~ ~

With the devil

Some people go to sleep with the devil
And wake up with the devil still in them
And then with the devil they run around all day
And if they don't flee from this evil and deceptive one
Then with the devil they will forever stay
With the devil

~ ~ ~

The Hardhead

She/he was a hardhead who would listen not
So she/he ended up in a place that was eternally hot
The Hardhead

Will You Ever Grow Up

Will you ever grow up or will you die a silly fool
Will you learn and discern your lessons of life
Or will you continue to create for yourself and for others
Unnecessary chaos, turmoil, trouble, toil, and strife
Will you ever grow up
How long will you continue to trod down the same old path
The path that leads to pain, suffering, and heartache
How long will you ignore the warning signs and signals
Will you heed the warning signs before it is too late
Will you ever grow up
Can't you see and can't you understand
That the harsh consequences that we sometimes must face
Are the direct results of the decisions that we make
Decisions that stem from the desires of our heart
Yet, we fail to realize just how much is really at stake
Will you ever grow up
For our actions and our reactions not only affect our lives
But they also affect the lives of so many others
Yes, in one way or another, our actions and our reactions
Affect the lives of our sisters and our brothers
Will you ever grow up
So, if the road that you are now on
Will not lead you to happiness, joy, and peace of mind
Then another road much different from the one you're on
Is the road that you should find
Will you ever grow up
For, the road that you're traveling on
Will continue to weigh and press you down
But heed the warning signs before it is too late
For the signs and signals are blaring all around
Will you ever grow up
Will you ever grow up or will you die a silly fool
Will you learn and discern your lessons of life
Or will you continue to create for yourself and for others
Unnecessary chaos, turmoil, trouble, toil, and strife
Will you ever grow up or will you die a silly fool
Will You Ever Grow Up

Life Can Hurt

Life can sometimes hurt
For, it is full of heartache, sorrow, trouble, and pain
Enough sometimes to shatter the human heart and rip it apart
Enough to drive the fragile human mind completely insane
But the Good News is that God is still a way-maker
And He has the power to lift us up and carry us safely through
And if only we call upon Him in both good times and bad
He will make a way out for me and for you
Because life can sometimes hurt
Life Can Hurt

~ ~ ~

Don't Do It

Don't do *"It"*
Whatever *"It"* may be
That on tomorrow
Will cause you regret, sadness, sorrow, and misery
So, don't do *"It"*
Whatever *"It"* may be
Don't Do It

~ ~ ~

Proper Nouns

Just to let you know, I do understand and realize
That proper nouns should always be capitalized
And in my poetry, this rule I do observe and obey
But when it comes to the names of satan the deceiver
Never, no, no, no, never shall I write them this way
For proper this evil manslayer is certainly not
And he will soon end up in a place that is eternally hot
So, as far as respecting him in my poetry, I will not
But just to let you know, I do understand and realize
That proper nouns should always be capitalized
Proper Nouns

Broken To Be Made Whole

Sometimes the Lord breaks us down in order to make us whole
Sometimes He allows chaos, conflict, and confusion in our lives
In order to help lift us up and save our very souls
Remember Jonah who didn't want to listen to the good Lord
When the Holy Spirit said unto him, "Jonah, go"
And how God caused him to be swallowed by a whale
Until a stronger spiritual sense of obedience Jonah came to know
Yes, the Lord broke Jonah down, so to speak
Until he became obedient and more spiritually sound
And remember Nebuchadnezzar the Babylonian king
Who refused to acknowledge the glory of the good Lord
Well, God took away his sanity for seven long years
And for seven long years, this king ate vegetation with the bulls
The Lord struck many throughout history with leprosy
And their skin turned as white as the driven snow
They were broken to be made whole
Until the glory of the Lord they came to personally know
Have you ever been broken down to be made whole
Maybe the devil is wreaking hell and havoc right now with your soul
Maybe you're going through, just came out of, or about to go in again
Whatever the case may be, please understand
God chastises, disciplines, molds, makes, and breaks those He loves
So that unto them, true blessings He shall rain down from above
So, through it all and no matter what
Hold tight to Jesus and He will fill and overflow your cup
For He has the power to deliver you and save your very soul
Even if it means breaking you down to make you whole
Broken To Be Made Whole

~ ~ ~

Break Me, Oh, Lord

Break me, oh, Lord, and make me the way that you want me to be
Yes, do whatever it takes, oh, Lord, even if it means breaking me
Break Me, Oh, Lord

Fix Me, Oh, Lord

Oh, Lord, I am but a broken vessel
So, please fix me, oh, Lord, the way you want me to be
Mix me, mold me, mend me, twist me, and bend me
Please, oh, please, Lord, do it for me
Whatever it shall take to get me closer to thee
For, close to you, oh, Lord, is where I want to be
So, fix me, oh, Lord, the way you want me to be
Fix Me, Oh, Lord

~ ~ ~

Please Work With Me Lord

Please work with me Lord
Please mold me and shape me just the way you want me to be
And, if from thee, oh, Lord, I try to run and hide
Because of my imperfect and human side
Then, like Jonah, who was cast into the raging and roaring sea
Please, oh, please, Lord, continue to work with me
Please discipline me as I need to be disciplined
For it is written that you discipline
Those whom you love so very much
May I learn and discern my lessons of life
And may my life and my living, Father, you forever touch
And thank you, Father, for loving me as you so lovingly do
Thank you for your mercy and for your grace
And thank you for your sweet compassion, too
For, there is no way that I could ever make it without you
Thank you for not giving up on me when I sometimes stray
Thank you for leading me and showing me the proper way
For these blessings, oh, Lord, I am truly thankful
Please Work With Me Lord

Things Happen

Things happen in our lives for many different reasons
Reasons that we must try to comprehend and figure out
Some reasons are simple and plain and some we cannot explain
Some are clear and some leave us in a state of confusion and doubt
But in everything that happens to us in life
The good, the bad, our struggles, and our strife
There are lessons to be learned
Lessons to comprehend, understand, and discern
Some lessons we learn indirectly from the lessons of others
Some lessons we learn directly on our own
Through the good times and the bad times
Through our ups and our downs and our turn-arounds
And if they don't kill us, they will help make us strong
Now, some people are stiff-necked and hardheaded
And refuse to learn their lessons well
Only to have to go through the fires of life once again
Only to have to once again go through the same old hell
Until they learn their lessons and learn them well
Things Happen

~ ~ ~

We All Go Through Something

We all go through something in one way or another
But believe me, my sisters and my brothers
We all go through something in one way or another
For no one can live upon the Earth at this time
And not be touched by troubles, heartaches, death, and dying
No, we all go through something in this old life
Yes, we will all experience some sort of sadness, sorrow, and strife
And with this point in mind, unto others, let us be nice and kind
For whether we like it or not
According to the Word, we are all true sisters and brothers
So, let's love one another, as we know we should
And let us remember to encourage and pray for each other
For, we all go through something in one way or another
We All Go Through Something

Come Inside   *Beverly Leonard*

When We Stray Away From the Word

When we stray away from the Word of the Lord
Our lives become uprooted, difficult, unbalanced, and rock-hard
A tangled web of confusion and a mixed-up mess
Our spirit becomes divided and unable to find peaceful rest
When we stray away from the Word of the Lord
We fall further and further behind
Collapsing and sinking into the sins of this old world
Filled with chaos, conflict, and confusion
Enough sometimes to blow the fragile human mind
When we stray away from the Word of the Lord
We try to find love in all the wrong places
And in the same company of those whom we keep
We find the same sad, confused, mixed-up, and miserable faces
When we stray away from the Word of the Lord
satan becomes the ruler of our hearts
Destroying any resemblance of what was once good in our lives
For when satan enters in, real love soon departs
When we stray away from the Word of the Lord
We will think, do, act, and say just about any and everything
Caring not for the feelings and the emotions of others
Nor for the heartaches and pains that our actions bring
When we stray away from the Word of the Lord
Our lives spin and spiral completely out of control
Doomed to end in death and destruction
Destined to destroy our very souls
When We Stray Away From the Word

~ ~ ~

Torn

We're torn between doing what is right and doing what is wrong
As the apostle Paul so wisely said so long ago, "Evil is always present"
Sitting on her twisted and demented throne
A constant battle between right and wrong
Please give me the strength, oh, Lord, to carry on
Torn

One More Time

Oh, Lord, can I talk to you one more time
For there's a lot of things, oh, Lord, that's on my mind
So, it's important that I talk to you one more time
For, only in your holy realm, true joy and peace I can find
So, please, oh, Lord, please, can I talk to you one more time
May I enter into your gates with thanksgiving and praise
May I kneel down before your holy and heavenly throne
And if need be, oh, Lord, please allow me
To weep, wail, cry out, shout, or just sit and moan
For sometimes life can be mighty difficult and hard
Sometimes so hard it makes me want to shout
Oh, my Lord, why, oh, why is my life so hard
But then I remember, oh, Lord, when you said in your Word
That you won't put anymore upon us than we can possibly bear
And that in times of ever-present trouble, oh, Lord
You said you'd make a way out and that you'd be right there
And I thank you, oh, Lord, right now for being right here
And allowing me to come into your holy presence so close and near
Thank you for your mercy, your grace, and for your listening ear
For now I am fortified and strengthened to go on from here
Thank you, oh, Lord, for giving me one more time
For the time that I spend with you, oh, Lord
Is always wonderful, refreshing, and so sublime
Thank you, oh, Lord, for giving me one more time
One More Time

~ ~ ~

Good Intentions

Good intentions are good, so please don't get me wrong
But good intentions are just not enough when they try to stand alone
For good intentions alone don't pay the utilities or the rent
They don't put food on the table or gas in the car
After the money is long gone, depleted, and spent
Yes, good intentions are good just as long as you can pay the rent
Good Intentions

Cluttered Living

Sometimes our lives can become too cluttered
Cluttered with material and monetary things
Too many baubles, beads, belts, and pins
Too many clothes, shoes, accessories, and rings
Too many debts, debits, and bills to pay
Making it a reality when they say
That the poorhouse is just one paycheck away
Too many responsibilities, deadlines, and duties
Too many irons in the fire and spread way too thin
Never a real moment of solitude and peace of mind
It makes you wonder when and if this madness will ever end
Too many worries, fears, dreads, and woes
They come in light dribbles and sometimes in heavy droves
Too many trials, tribulations, troubles, and pains
Enough to cause the mind to snap and go completely insane
Too many relationships not relating
Too many associates who are only hating
Too many so-called friends who will stab you in your back
For the moment your back is turned
Will be the moment they will attack
Too many doctrines, beliefs, and philosophies
Which can easily clutter and confuse the human mind
For in Mankind's search for questions left unanswered
Mixed-up madness, mayhem, and confusion is what many do find
So, there come times in our lives
The need to streamline or completely rid ourselves
Of unnecessary and negative things that weigh us down
Things, situations, people, and circumstances
That keep us straddled to the cold hard ground
Yes, there come times in our lives
The need to streamline or completely rid ourselves
Of unnecessary and negative things that weigh us down
Have you streamlined and cleaned out your life lately
Maybe it's that time once again
Cluttered Living

Please Walk With Me Lord

As I walk through the valley of the shadow of death
Please walk with me Lord
For this old world can get mighty difficult and downright hard
So, please, oh, please, walk with me Lord
For I cannot walk this journey alone
I need you, oh, Lord, to lead, guide, protect, and make me strong
So, please, oh, please, walk with me Lord
And please bless me with what I need to carry on
As I walk through the valley of the shadow of death
Please walk with me Lord
Please Walk With Me Lord

~ ~ ~

Fear and Doubt

Fear and doubt are serial killers
For they maim and destroy everywhere they strike
They creep in, break down, demolish, devastate, and destroy
Sending shallow and weak faith fast and furious into flight
For if your faith is weak
Fear and doubt will surely creep
Into your innermost psychic mind
Armed with lies, deceit, disillusions, and confusions
And soon faith or any resemblance of it
You will no longer find
Fear and doubt have devastated and destroyed
Many souls many times before
For one weak moment alone with these killers
Have left many weakened to the very core
So, be aware and beware of these serial killers
For they seek to destroy your very life
Then leave you in a losing state
Filled with pain, suffering, heartache, and strife
Be aware and beware of these serial killers
Fear and Doubt

Swimming In Mud Going Up-Stream

Sometimes it seems as if we're swimming in mud going up-stream
Sometimes so dense, dark, and thick it makes us want to scream
Sometimes it seems as if we're swimming in mud going up-stream
But we've got to keep on swimming until we reach the top
We can't give up, give in, give out, nor can we ever stop
We must trudge on and endure until the very end
If, in Paradise with the Lord, we hope to eternally spend
So, we must tell the muddy waters
"Muddy waters move on out of our way
We shall not allow you to hold us back today"
Yes, when hard times come like they always do
We must keep on swimming up-stream until we make it on through
Swimming In Mud Going Up-Stream

~ ~ ~

Some Days

Some days are good and some days are bad
Some days we wish we never had
But in order to get to the days that are good
We've got to go through the days that are bad
Some Days

~ ~ ~

Life Will Make You Cry Sometimes

Life will make you cry sometimes
For just as surely as the day you were born
As you live your life upon the Earth
Your heart will be broken, shattered, pierced, and torn
Yes, life will make you cry sometimes
Just as surely as the day you were born
Life Will Make You Cry Sometimes

Trouble Drops Like Rain

```
T        d        l        r
 r        r        i        a
  o        o        k        i
   u        p        e        n
    b        s
     l
      e
```

On my windowpane
Enough sometimes to make a weaker mind
Snap and go completely insane
Yes, trouble drops like rain on my windowpane
And it seems when one problem is solved along comes two
Pouring down so hard sometimes, I don't know what to do
But through the storms of life I must hold on
I must not give up, give in, or give out
No, through turbulent times I must be strong
And upon the Lord's holy name, I shall continue to call
For He strengthens, encourages, and fortifies me
And helps lift me up quickly when I sometimes fall
Yes, upon the Lord's holy name I shall continue to call
Despite the dark clouds, the raging storms, and the rain
That constantly drops on my windowpane

```
D        d        d        d
r        r        r        r
i        i        i        i
p        p        p        p
```

Trouble Drops Like Rain

~ ~ ~

I Cry a Million Tears

I cry a million tears
To wash away the pains, the heartaches, and the fears
Yes, I cry a million tears
I Cry a Million Tears

Come Inside   *Beverly Leonard*

The Tears Nobody Know

Sometimes when I'm all alone and by myself
When there's nobody around but me and the Lord
Sometimes I cry a river of tears
A flow long, deep, heavy, and hard
These are the tears nobody know
Nobody but me and the Lord
I cry when my burdens are compounded and seem to overflow
I cry when I don't know which way to turn or which way to go
I cry when my body aches and throbs with great pain
I cry when I see my people selling our people out for greedy gain
I cry when, by those I love the most, I am lied to and deceived
I cry when I see children not getting the love they deserve to receive
I cry when children lack great shame, honor, and respect
But when I look at the trees from whence they fell
What more should I really expect
I cry when death comes calling on my family, friends, and kin
I cry for the innocent lives lost in the bloody wars of men
I cry for Black mothers who are tired, weary, and weak
For no matter how hard they try to make the two ends meet
Life tries even harder to knock them off their tired feet
I cry for the Black man who has been beaten and bashed
And treated far worse than an old tin can
I cry when I see what has happened to the Black family clan
Shattered, battered, and scattered all over the land
I cry for my beautiful Black people who were brutally enslaved
For its negative effects can still be felt down to this very day
I cry when I see injustices done to my fellow man
I cry because doers of evil are running rampant all over the land
I cry when I see Mankind's tendency to dominate one another
It's man against man and brother against brother
Yes, sometimes when I'm all alone and by myself
When there's nobody around but me and the Lord
Sometimes I cry a river of tears
A river long, deep, heavy, and hard
These are the tears nobody know
Nobody but me and the Lord
The Tears Nobody Know

I Know I'm Getting Older

I know I'm getting older
Because some of the things that I use to do
Either I can't or I desire not to do them anymore
For, I'm on a different path than the path I was on before
Besides, the older I get, the closer I get to Heaven's door
May I continue on the path that I'm now on
And I pray that it will one day lead me to my heavenly home
Yes, I know I'm getting older but that's all right with me
Just as long as I have Jesus who died to set me free
I Know I'm Getting Older

~ ~ ~

A Very Scary Thought

It's a very scary thought to think that there may come a time
When precious memories will begin to fade from my mind
Yes, it's a very scary thought to think that one day
Precious memories that I once treasured may fade away
So, I pray that with me my memories shall always stay
But if one day my memories start to fade away. . .
Oh, well, what can I say
I don't look forward to that day
A Very Scary Thought

~ ~ ~

The Laughter

The memories were fading from her mind fast
The short-termed ones just didn't last
So, I told her, "Mother, you must remember what to remember"
She laughed, then I laughed
Both knowing that she would not remember
What to remember to remember
But we laughed that day
I will remember the laughter
The Laughter

Gray Hair

Gray hair seems to have a life of its own
And no matter how you try to color, tint, and/or dye it
The gray always comes back ever so strong
I might as well leave my gray hair along
Gray Hair

~ ~ ~

Old Folks and Bifocals

As a kid I thought that bifocals
Were only for old folks
Well, I now wear bifocals
So, I guess that makes me an old folk
Old Folks and Bifocals

~ ~ ~

Looking For Patience

As I get older, my patience gets shorter
So, I'm looking for patience
Tell me, have you seen her
For I need her to help me deal with
The people, the situations, and the circumstances in my life
That, without patience, would no doubt cause me
Great frustration, irritation, stress, stain, and strife
So, I'm looking for patience
To help me deal with the difficulties of this old life
So, if by chance you happen to see her
Please send her quickly my way
For I need lots of patience each and every day
Looking For Patience

There Will Always Be Somebody

There will always be somebody
Who will try to bring you down
There will always be somebody
Who will try to bring you to the ground
There will always be somebody
Who will try to steal your peace and joy
And because they're not happy with their own lives
Your life they will seek to destroy
There will always be somebody
With hurtful and unkind things to say
Spewing words like poisoned arrows
Trying to take your happiness and joy away
There will always be somebody
Trying to pull your spirit down
With their mean and rude and negative attitude
They'll try to pull your spirit to the ground
There will always be somebody
Who will try to use, misuse, and abuse you
Taking your kindness as a sign of mere weakness
They'll try to put the squeeze right onto you
There will always be somebody
Who will try to bring shame to your name
For whatever benefits they can possibly reap
For selfish gain is what these kinds of people seek
There will always be somebody
Spreading vicious rumors about your life
Sowing seeds of deceit and untruths
Creating for you unnecessary stresses, strains, and strife
There will always be somebody
Who will try to stab you in your back
And the moment you let your guard down
Will be the moment they will attack
There will always be somebody
Who will try to bring you down
There will always be somebody
Who will try to bring you to the ground
There Will Always Be Somebody

If You Think You've Got It Bad

If you think you've got it bad
You'd better take a good look around
For there are others who are far worse off than you are
Who must live and sleep on the cold hard ground
Yes, if you think you've got it bad
You'd better open up your eyes and see
All the turmoil and trouble in this troubled world
All the suffering, pain, heartache, and misery
If you think you've got it bad
You'd better listen carefully with discerning ears
And you'll notice that the conversations of this world
Are compounded by worry, stress, sadness, chaos, and fears
For many people around the world simply know not
How they're going to make it from one day to another
For there's poverty, violence, corruption, and strife
It's man against man and brother against brother
And if by the divine grace and mercy of the good Lord
That you keep on living upon the Earth
Situations and circumstances are sure to become even worse
For the prophecies are now being realized and fulfilled
Yes, life and living will seem to be one huge curse
So, instead of sitting around criticizing and complaining
About how terrible your life has become
You'd better take a close and personal look around
And realize that your life is truly a blessed one
If You Think You've Got It Bad

~ ~ ~

Less Is Sometimes Best

Less is sometimes best
Just as long as we have the essential things
For why hold on to unneeded and unnecessary 'stuff'
And to all the chaos and confusion the unnecessary 'stuff' brings
Yes, sometimes less is best
Just as long as we have the essential things
Less Is Sometimes Best

Money Doesn't Come Easy

As a child, I would often hear my parents say
That money doesn't come easy, nor from trees does it grow
Well, I can now appreciate their words of true wisdom
For the meaning of this old saying, I have indeed come to know
For now, I am a parent raising three children of my own
And I now know first hand just how hard it can be
Trying to maintain and provide for a family and a home
So, when my precious children ask for this, that, or the other
I fondly recall the wise words of my dear father and mother
And with a sincere heart, the words seem to flow with such ease
As I explain to my own dear and darling children
That money doesn't come easy, nor does it grow on trees
Money Doesn't Come Easy

~ ~ ~

By Candlelight

By candlelight we come together as one
By candlelight we create our own made-up fun
By candlelight we sing and tell stories and jokes
By candlelight we eat together like normal-acting folks
By candlelight we talk into the wee hours of the night
Until it's time to blow out the candle lights
But not before saying our prayers to the good Lord
And thanking Him for the candles when times are hard
By Candlelight

~ ~ ~

You Don't Have To Look Far

You don't have to look far to find trouble
In fact, looking for trouble is something you really don't have to do
For trouble has its very own ways of successfully finding you
But through all of your troubles, trials, tribulations, and strife
Remember, too, you don't have to look far to find Jesus Christ
You Don't Have To Look Far

Speak the Words

If you want something bad enough
You've got to speak the words
And let them out into the universe
If you want something bad enough
Speak the Words

~ ~ ~

I Speak These Words

I speak these words out into the universe
Love
Joy
Happiness
Harmony
Tranquility
Peace
Serenity
Goodwill
Family
Home
Health
Prosperity
Community
Commitment
Fellowship
Friendship
Brotherhood
Sisterhood
Honor
Respect
Compassion
Forgiveness
Sharing
Caring
Prayer
Hope
Salvation
I speak these words out into the universe
I Speak These Words

Come Inside *Beverly Leonard*

I waited patiently for the Lord
He turned to me and He heard my cry
He lifted me out of the slimy pit
Out of the mud and mire
He set my feet on a rock
And gave me a firm place to stand
He put a new song in my mouth
A hymn of praise to our God

Psalms 40:1-3

Chapter Three
Words of Encouragement

As A Friend

As a friend
I must tell you that there is a God who loves and cares for you so
And that to Him for anything and everything
You can always freely go
Yes, as a friend, I must tell you
That there is a God who loves and cares for you so
As a friend
I must tell you of the glorious hope that God has given to all Mankind
It is the hope of life-ever-after beyond this earthly plane
And that another hope so glorious and grand we cannot find
Yes, as a friend, I must tell you
Of the glorious hope that God has given to all Mankind
As a friend
I must tell you that we must live our lives according to God's Word
Or that into the eternal flames our spirits shall be hurled
Yes, as a friend I must tell you
That we must live our lives according to God's Holy Word
And not live according to the prince of this wicked old world
As a friend
Please know that I love and care for you so
And that I want the best for you now and in the future to come
So that when this earthly life is over, said, and done
Together we'll stand proudly as friends with the Most Holy One
Yes, as a friend
Please know that I love and care for you so
And that from the bottom of my heart
These things I want you to know
As A Friend

~ ~ ~

You Are My Friend

You are my friend through thick and through thin
And friends we shall continue to be
Now and throughout eternity
You Are my Friend

Another Day

The Lord has blessed you to see another day
Another day to teeter, totter, stagger, and sway
Or another day in God's Holy Word to strive to stay
Another day to be depressed, downhearted, sullen, and sad
Or another day to rejoice in the day that God gave and in it be glad
Another day to be angry, irate, disappointed, and upset
Or another day to be happy and appreciate all the blessings you get
Another day to be impolite, ill mannered, discourteous, and rude
Or another day to display a kind spirit and a positive attitude
Another day to be selfish and fail to lend a helping hand
Or another day to care and share and help lift your fellow man
Another day to be arrogant, boisterous, haughty, and proud
Or another day to be humble, meek, modest, and mild
Another day to bring to yourself honor, praise, and glory
Or another day to lift God's name, for He is still almighty and holy
Another day to gossip and sow negative seeds into the ground
Or another day to help spread love, joy, and hope all around
Another day to steal, cheat, lie, and kill
Or another day to obey God's commandments and do His holy will
Another day to consume alcohol or be a crazed-out drug fiend
Or another day to celebrate being sane, sober, and clean
Another day to flee from the Lord, though from Him we cannot go
Or another day of His goodness and His glory to come to know
Another day to keep the Good News of God's Kingdom to yourself
Or another day to share the Good News with someone else
Yes, the Lord has blessed you to see another day
Now, how will you chose to live it
Another Day

~ ~ ~

To Him We Can Go

In times of trials, tribulations, troubles, and woe
To our heavenly Father we can always freely go
For He is always there in both good times and bad
He lifts our spirits and comforts our souls
And He makes our hearts happy and glad
To Him We Can Go

Each Day

Each day is a blessing
Granted to us by the good Lord above
Because of His goodness, His mercy, and His undying love
A love so great, wonderful, and kind
Another love like it we cannot find
Each day is a blessing

Each day is a challenge
For each day has its very own troubles, ills, and woes
Sometimes they come in light dribbles
Sometimes they overwhelm us in heavy droves
Each day is a challenge

Each day is an opportunity
To form a close and personal relationship with the Lord
To live, to learn, to love, and to up-lift one another
To help spread peace and joy to our sisters and our brothers
Each day is an opportunity

Thank you, Heavenly Father, for this day
And thank you for loving me in an awesome way
Please give me the strength to carry on
And when I feel burdened down by the troubles of this world
Please lift me up and help make me strong
Please lead me, guide me, and show me the proper way
And by my side, Lord, please, oh, please, stay
And as I walk this earthly journey
Please continue to bless and keep me
So that I may be a blessing to others
Please pour your Holy Spirit down upon me, Father
So that I may help up-lift and encourage
My sisters and my brothers

For each day is a blessing
Each day is a challenge
Each day is an opportunity
Each Day

A Brand New Day

The Lord blessed you to see a brand new day
And the choice is yours as to how you will make use of it
Whether you will walk with the Lord throughout the day
Or whether from the good Lord you shall fall astray
Whether you will moan, groan, criticize, and complain
About the way things are going or not going in your life
Or whether you will thank the Lord for all that He has done
And pray that He will continue to bless and keep you
And help you through your trials, your tribulations, and strife
Whether you will use this day to learn something new
Something that will enhance your life and your living, too
Whether wisdom, knowledge, and understanding you shall find
Or whether this day will slip by without expanding your mind
Whether you will use this day to help someone along life's way
By extending a helping hand to help up-lift your fellow man
Whether you will share the Good News of the Lord with others
Or cause harm and devastation to your sisters and brothers
Yes, the good Lord blessed you to see a brand new day
Now, use it wisely, this I pray
A Brand New Day

~ ~ ~

The Right Time Called Today

I'm not as young as I used to be
Nor am I as old as I hope to become one day
Therefore, I'm just where I need to be
I'm at the right time in my life called Today
Therefore, today, I shall not look back with regrets
Nor shall I worry about that which has yet to be
For this is the day the Lord has made
I shall rejoice in it and give God the praise and the glory
The Right Time Called Today

Don't Forget to Bless Others

Remember, to whom much is given, much is expected
And to whom much more is given, much more is expected
So, whatever blessings you receive in life
Make sure you give that much in return
For, the Giver of all blessings is watching from Heaven above
So, make sure these lessons on giving you truly discern
Don't Forget to Bless Others

~ ~ ~

Before His Holy Throne

If there is something pressing heavily upon your heart and mind
Please allow me to direct you to the holy throne of the Lord
And true peace and joy your soul shall refreshingly find
If there is something pressing and weighing heavily upon your mind
For this old world is full of heartache, suffering, and sorrow
But please know that God is our Rock in a weary land
And our hope for a better and brighter today and tomorrow
Therefore, whatever it is that is causing your mind to be in a bind
Please take it to the Lord and believe in your heart
That everything is going to work out and turn out just fine
And remember that God himself said
That He would never put anymore upon us than we can bare
And that He will always leave a way out of every bind
So, if there is something pressing and weighing heavily on your mind
Whatever it is take it to the Lord in prayer and leave it there
Leave it before His holy throne
Before His Holy Throne

Come Inside   *Beverly Leonard*

Make Each Moment Count

We're here on the Earth for only a short period of time
For, like the fresh morning dew, we'll soon fade away
So, while we are here, we must make each moment count
For upon this Earth we shall not always stay

We must not take for granted our family and friends
Those who are dear and precious to our hearts
And with a smile, we must greet every stranger we meet
So that love and caring shall never die or depart

We must make each moment count in the lives of our children
For our children are true gifts from the good Lord above
So, we must enjoy the times that we have with our children
While teaching and training them in God's holy and divine love

For, all too soon, our children will be grown-ups themselves
With families and homes of their own
So, make the moments count that you share with your children
And create for them a caring, loving, safe, and happy home

We must make each moment count
As we build strong and lasting relationships
With God as well as with our fellow man
Then our hope for the future will shine as brightly as the sun
Once our lives on the Earth are over, said, and done

We must drop the anger and cease the bitterness
As well as the hatred toward our fellow man
We must put racism and prejudice in their proper places
And walk this Earth peacefully hand in hand

So, make each and every moment count each and every day
With God as our leader guiding us along the way
For, if we live in love, true blessings will flow from above
So, let us make each moment count starting today
Make Each Moment Count

Into My Little Room

Into my little room I often go
To be by myself and in the holy presence of the good Lord
And into my little room, I carry all of my burdens
When life becomes overwhelming, difficult, and rock-hard
And like a loving Father, He is always there to receive me
To comfort me during these troubling times of sorrow and woe
And because I can lay all of my burdens down before Him
Into my little room I often go
For He hears my cries and He sees my tears
He feels my pains and He knows all of my frets and fears
Sometimes I sit quietly without saying a word
And the Holy Spirit speaks and intercedes for me
And that which is unspoken is soon made known and heard
And the Lord gives me the courage to continue on
He lifts me up, fortifies me, and He makes me strong
So that when I emerge from my little room
I am equipped with the necessities to carry on
And when the times come back around
When I again become burdened down by stress and strife
I shall return quickly to my little room
To be in the holy presence of the good Lord
Who is the Giver, the Receiver, and the Restorer of life
Into My Little Room

~ ~ ~

The devil Has Already Been Defeated

Hallelujah, the devil has already been defeated
Beaten down, overcome, conquered, crushed, tossed out, and up-seated
For, you see, this manslayer never had a chance to take God's place
And now he's mad as hell and eagerly seeks to destroy the human race
But let us stand firm in the Word and listen not to this evil one
Let us command him to get behind us in the mighty name of Jesus
God's only begotten Son
Hallelujah, the devil has already been defeated
The devil Has Already Been Defeated

Cling To Your Faith

When life seems much too hard to bare
When it seems as if there is no one who really cares
When the world seems to be crashing down all around you
Please remember that God is right there
And that He can and will see you safely through
For the Lord said that He would not place anymore upon us
Than we can possibly bare
Therefore, whatever it is that you are going through
The Lord has said that you can make it
For He has already made a way out for you
But because we are mere human mortals
We fail to see what is coming up around the bend
And because we sometimes fail to cling to our faith
When hard times come, we think that our lives are about to end
But cling to your faith and hold onto it tightly
And never, never, never, never let it slip away
For true joy and peace are found only in the Lord
And life outside of His Word is extremely difficult and rock-hard
So, cling to your faith and it shall elevate and lift you up
It shall lift you up and out of your depressive state of mind
And this is not to say that life will be easy, for life is hard
But great comfort and strength are found in the good Lord
And listen not to the evil and deceitful one
The one who pursues us when our spirits are weary and weak
Listen not to the one who tries to bring ruin and devastation
For the hearts and souls of Mankind this manslayer seeks
Cling to your faith and call upon the Lord's holy name
For, after all this time, He still loves us just the same
Cling to your faith and cling to it both night and day
And the grand Creator who created the Heavens and the Earth
For you will make a way
Cling To Your Faith

Where Is Your Faith

Troubles, trials, and tribulations were trying to get me down
They sought to overwhelm me and level me to the ground
But in the midst of it all
When satan was trying his best to test me and make me fall
I had to step outside of myself and check myself
And ask myself, "Where, oh, where is my faith"
Yes, I had to step outside of myself and check myself
To see if my faith was really in place
For, oh, how easy it is to say when everything is going our way
That our faith is firmly rooted and is securely in place
But what about those times when times get down-right hard
So hard sometimes it makes you want to shout
"Oh, my Lord, why, oh, why, is my life so hard"
Yes, I had to step outside of myself
And ask myself where is my faith
But through it all, I've come to find out
That it is in times like these when life tries to knock us to our knees
That we come to know what God's goodness and mercy is all about
If we just keep the faith when troubles come barreling our way
And believe in our hearts that joy will come at the break of day
Where Is Your Faith

~ ~ ~

I'm Pressing On

I'm pressing on toward my heavenly home
For my journey down here is nearing its earthly end
Then my new spiritual journey shall begin
But until that time comes
When I'll return to my heavenly home
Upon the Earth, I'll continue to press on
I'm Pressing On

Keep the Faith

When the troubles of this old world come crashing down upon you
When you can't make the two ends meet no matter what you do
When you feel like calling it quits and giving up on life
Because of your trials, your troubles, your tribulations, and strife
Remember what the Lord said when it feels like you're in sinking sand
He said He would never place anymore upon us than we can stand
Therefore, whatever it is that you are going through
Whatever it is that has been placed upon you
You must remember, that for you, God has already made a way out
He said it, and you must believe it without a shadow of a doubt
So, when the troubles of this old world
Seem to be getting the best of you
And it seems that you have nowhere to run and no one to turn to
Turn to God and hold on tight
For He alone can turn our darkness into glorious light
Trust in God and He will see you through
Keep the faith no matter what is placed upon you
For hard times will come like they always do
But trust in the Lord and He will see you safely through
When the troubles of this old world come crashing down upon you
You must keep the faith
Keep the Faith

~ ~ ~

Let Me Encourage You

Let me encourage you to continue on
May my words of encouragement
Help lift you up, brighten your day, and help make you strong
May they touch your heart, mind, and soul in a special way
May my words of encouragement encourage you today
Let Me Encourage You

Faith Is Like Falling

Having faith is like *f*
       a
       l
      l
       i
       n
       g
From a place that is lofty, high, and tall
Yet, believing without a shadow of a doubt
That a safety net lies below to catch you if you fall
Faith Is Like Falling

~ ~ ~

Believe In Yourself

You must believe in yourself and in your ability to succeed
Or you won't make it very far in this old life
For if you fail to believe that you can soar high like an eagle
You'll be consumed with fear, worry, doubt, stress, and strife
Along with low self-esteem, self-pity, and a lack of self-respect
Yes, if you fail to believe in yourself, this is what you should expect
For you'll never come to know what self-confidence is all about
Strike one, strike two, strike three, life will knock you out
So, you must believe in yourself without a shadow of a doubt
And listen not to those who say that you cannot achieve
But in yourself and in your abilities you must always believe
Yes, believe in your heart that you are a special and blessed soul
And always look to the One who created you beautiful and whole
For then and only then shall your true blessings unfold
Believe In Yourself

~ ~ ~

Be Comfortable In Your Own Skin

Be comfortable in your own skin
Whatever color, shape, or size you may happen to be in
Be comfortable in your own skin
Be Comfortable In Your Own Skin

Facing the Fears

Anxiety woke me up this morning
Banging at my door
It wouldn't let me eat
It wouldn't let me sleep
It wouldn't let me run anymore
So, there she stood before me
Staring me straight in my eyes
She said I must face my fears
And face them head on
Or I would surely die
Well, I wasn't ready to die yet
For there was more of life to see
Places to go and things to do
Besides, my children really needed me
So, I took a good look at my problems
For they had not disappeared
And with a prayer and a plan, I took command
And began to conquer that which I feared
Facing the Fears

~ ~ ~

Face It and Fix It

The preacher said just the other day
"You can't fix '**It**' if you don't face '**It**'
Whatever the '**It**' may be
Whatever '**It**' is that is causing you pain and misery"
Yes, the preacher said this just the other day
And it made perfect sense to me
For, if we fail to face our fears and face them head on
Then, like a raisin in the sun
Our spirit and our joy will whither away and be gone
But the sooner we face '**It**', whatever the '**It**' may be
The sooner we will be able to enjoy peace of mind and serenity
So, let us face '**It**' and fix '**It**'
Whatever '**It**' may be
Face It and Fix It

Be Thankful

Be thankful for family and also for friends
Be thankful for good neighbors, co-workers, and kin
Be thankful for the roof that covers your head
Be thankful for the ability to rise and get out of bed
Be thankful for the bed in which to rest and lay your head
Be thankful for your daily bread
Be thankful for the clothes that you have on your back
Be thankful in times of plenty and also in times of lack
Be thankful for the beautiful and bountiful Earth
Be thankful that God gave unto Mankind a blessed birth
Be thankful for the wonderful gift of life
Be thankful that God gave us his Son Jesus Christ
Be thankful for the cross on Calvary
Be thankful that Jesus died for you and for me
Be thankful that from the grips of hell He set us free
Be thankful He wiped our sins away
Be thankful that He rose from the cross on the third day
Be thankful for the Holy Spirit He lovingly left behind
Be thankful for His holy and inspired Word
For in it truth, wisdom, and salvation we all can find
Be thankful that God has not forgotten that we came from dust
Be thankful that He still loves and cares for us
Be thankful to have the things that you have
And be thankful for the things that you have but know not
For God blesses us in more ways than we will ever know
Yes, the good Lord blesses us with a whole lot
So, be thankful for what you've got
Be Thankful

~ ~ ~

Don't Let an Opportunity Pass by Today

Don't let an opportunity pass by today
To help lift, encourage, or inspire someone along life's way
For what goes around will surely come back around one day
Don't Let an Opportunity Pass by Today

Come Inside *Beverly Leonard*

Count It as a Blessing

When you wake up and see a brand new day
Count it as a blessing
When you have a bed in which to rest and your head to lay (lie)
Count it as a blessing
When you're able to rise out of bed and stand on your own two feet
Count it as a blessing
When you have nourishing and enough food in which to eat
Count it as a blessing
When you're able to feed yourself all by yourself
Count it as a blessing
When you have shoes to wear and clothes to put on your back
Count it as a blessing
When times are good and troubles and trials you temporarily lack
Count it as a blessing
When you have a job or receive funds to help you pay your bills
Count it as a blessing
When you have medicine to take when you're sick and feeling ill
Count it as a blessing
When you have money for gas to put in your car
Count it as a blessing
When you have bus fare or the ability to walk if you must walk far
Count it as a blessing
If you have a loving family and a home where you feel that you belong
Count it as a blessing
If you have been blessed with children and grandchildren of your very own
Count it as a blessing
If you have or had parents who are rearing or have properly raised you well
Count it as a blessing
If you have people in your life who encourages you to prosper and excel
Count it as a blessing
If you have true friends who'll stick by you through thick and through thin
Count it as a blessing
If your hair turns gray and your eyes begin to dim
Count it as a blessing
If your name is called and your spirit returns to the Lord's holy realm
Count it as a blessing
For, when we start counting our blessings, we will clearly see
Just how good God is to you and to me when we count our blessings
Count It as a Blessing

In Times Like These

When life gets you down and troubles abound
And everything seems to be going wrong
Reach out to the good Lord and onto Him hold on
And, like eagles, He will lift you up and make you strong
In times like these
When your bills are piling high and your money is sinking low
And it seems there is no one you can turn to or for help you can go
In times like these, go to the Lord
For He can make ways out when times are difficult and hard
In times like these
When others forsake, disappoint, abandon, and let you down
And in them no mercy and compassion can be found
In times likes these, depend upon the Lord instead
For in Him abundant love, mercy, and grace abound
In times like these
When you lose someone you love
And your heart is bereaved and broken in two
Lean upon the good Lord for He will not let you fall
He will strengthen you and help you make it through
In times like these
When you're feeling feeble, tired, weary, worn, and weak
In times like these, it's Jesus whom you should seek
For you can call upon Him and He will catch you if you fall
And lift you up and place you firmly on your feet
In times like these
When your spirit is held hostage by evil and demonic spirits
Which can come through alcoholic and mind-altering drugs
That turn their victims into sad, demented, and dangerous thugs
Call on Jesus and from this hell He will pull you out
For salvation from any and everything is what Jesus is all about
In times like these
When things happen in your life and you don't understand why
Lean not on your own understanding, but know that God is in control
And that He has brought you thus far and He'll never leave you alone
And that He still loves and cares for your very soul
In times like these
In Times Like These

Come Inside *Beverly Leonard*

Stay In the Light

When life overwhelms and burdens you down
Stay in the light
When joy and peace of mind cannot be found
Stay in the light
When troubles and sorrows come your way
Stay in the light
When these same troubles and sorrows seem to want to stay
Stay in the light
When your so-called friends turn their backs on you
Stay in the light
When those you can depend upon are way too few
Stay in the light
When others treat you unkindly and are mean and rude
Stay in the light
When you want to scream and shout, "I give up. I'm through"
Stay in the light
When others talks behind your back
Stay in the light
When your reputation, feelings, and emotions are under attack
Stay in the light
When those you love fail to love you back
Stay in the light
When true caring and compassion are what you lack
Stay in the light
When trials, tribulations, and temptations come your way
Stay in the light
When satan tries to snatch your soul by causing you to stray
Stay in the light
For, in the light, true joy and peace can be found
And everything outside of the light
Keeps us leveled and straddled to the cold, hard ground
Remember, when all hell breaks loose
Stay in the light
Stay In the Light

Just Pray

When the storms of life rant and rage all around you
Just pray
When it seems as if there is nothing more that you can do
Just pray
When you've done your best and it seems your best isn't enough
Just pray
When times get difficult and hard and the road gets tough
Just pray
When those you depend upon turn their backs on you
Just pray
When it seems there's nowhere to run and no one to turn to
Just pray
When your so-called friends talk behind your back
Just pray
When your feelings and emotions are both under attack
Just pray
When satan tries to tempt you and destroy your very soul
Just pray
When your dreams and your goals fail to unfurl and unfold
Just pray
When fear, dread, and doubt creep into your mind
Just pray
When joy and peace of mind you cannot find
Just pray
When troubles, trials, and tribulations come your way
Just pray
Because prayer has the power to turn things around
Through prayer, real joy and peace in the Lord can be found
We need only to ask the Lord with a sincere and honest heart
And He who created the Heavens and also the Earth
Shall grant us blessed beginnings and brand new starts
He will refreshen our souls and lighten our loads
If we just pray
Just pray

Prayer and Meditation

Prayer and meditation is a two way conversation
For when we pray, we talk to the Lord
And He listens to us with discerning ears
As we tell Him all about our problems, our joys, and our fears
And when we meditate, the Lord speaks to us and we listen to Him
As He teaches, leads, and guides us in His holy and righteous realm
Yes, prayer and meditation is a two way conversation
Therefore, let us not be so swift, hasty, or quick
To walk away right after we pray
But let us take time out to meditate
And hear what the Lord may say
Prayer and Meditation

~ ~ ~

A Little Push

Sometimes in life, we need a little push to help us along life's way
For sometimes, our way can get awfully dismal, dark, and dreary
Causing our spirits to get tired, weak, worn out, and weary
Therefore, sometimes in life we need a little push
Maybe a helping hand to help lift our spirit higher
Maybe a kind word to comfort, encourage, and inspire us
Maybe a gentle embrace, a tender hug, a kiss, or a smile
Maybe a high five to help us walk those extra miles
Yes, sometimes in life we need a little push
And sometimes in life, we must push others along life's way
To help our sisters and brothers have a better and brighter day
We must sometimes lend a helping hand and help others to stand
We must be merciful, loving, gentle, compassionate, and kind
So that in our hearts on that great day great love the Lord shall find
For love covers a multitude of sins and sinners all are we
But by the blood of Jesus, from sin we are all set free
Therefore, may we be blessed to be pushed along life's way
And may we bless others as we push them along, this I pray
A Little Push

Struggling Lady

Struggling Lady struggles each day to survive
Trying her very best and then some
To nurture, protect, maintain, train, and provide
Working overtime trying to make a dollar and a dime
To feed and clothe her children and pay her bills on time
But as hard as she tries to make the two ends meet
Life seems to try even harder to knock Struggling Lady off her feet
But Struggling Lady knows that if she falls she must quickly rise
Dust herself off and dry her weeping eyes
For Struggling Lady sometimes moan, cry, weep, and wail
As she struggles through life's heartaches, pains, hurts, and hells
And into her cocoon, her quiet room, Struggling Lady often goes
And like the great river Nile in Africa's land
Her tears, worries, frets, and fears burst forth and overflow
As she sing praises to her Creator and purges her often weary soul
Struggling Lady prays each and every day
Asking the Lord to please lead, guide, and bless her along the way
And always for others Struggling Lady always pray
Knowing that if she holds on to God's unchanging hands
There shall surely come a better and brighter day
For her faith in the Lord is strong
And upon the Lord, Struggling Lady has learned
To lean, trust, call, and depend upon
For, you see, life hasn't killed Struggling Lady
On the contrary, it has made her strong
So, hold your head up high, Struggling Lady
Trudge on, be strong, and endure until the very end
Don't give up, give in, or give out, Struggling Lady
So that with the Lord in Paradise you shall forever spend
Struggling Lady

~ ~ ~

Keep Your Head Up

Keep your head up when the goings get rough
And remember to constantly call upon the good Lord
And He will help you make it through when times get hard
Keep Your Head Up

Come Inside   *Beverly Leonard*

You Must Continue On

One foot in front and then the other
You must continue on
Or life will pass right over you
And your hopes, your dreams, and your future will all be gone
For no matter how hard the problems seem
There are solutions to them all
So, don't give up the battle called Life
And get up quickly if you stumble and fall
For even though today may be stormy, dark, and cloudy
There will be sunshine and warmth tomorrow
And a beautiful rainbow to lift you up
And help you through your pains and all of your sorrows
So, one foot in front and then the other
You must continue on
You Must Continue On

~ ~ ~

For Ourselves

As wives, mothers, daughters, sisters
Aunts, good neighbors, friends, and kin
We do so many things for others
For our husbands, our children, our parents
Our siblings, our kinfolk, and our friends
Even strangers that we happen to meet on the street
We try to inspire them and lift them to their feet
But we must learn to take time out and do for ourselves
Or we will be unable to do anything for anyone else
If we fail to take time out and care for ourselves
So, let us take time out for ourselves and grow spiritually strong
For the Word of the Lord will strengthen us and help us to hold on
It is an anchor unto our feet and a light to lead the way
And with the Lord on our side we shall not lose or fall astray
Let us take time for ourselves and enjoy each and every day
For Ourselves

Mama's Got to Make It

Mama's got to make it for her kids and for herself
Because other than the good Lord above
She really can't depend on anyone else
Yes, mama's got to make it for her kids and for herself
So she labors at work trying to make the two ends meet
But as hard as she tries to maintain and survive
Life tries even harder to knock her off her feet
But mama knows that she can't afford to stay down
Mama knows that if she stumbles and falls
She must quickly rise from the cold hard ground
So she toils and she strives each day to do her very best
To feed, clothe, protect, and provide for her family
Realizing that each day is yet another trial and test
But her faith in the good Lord is strong
And mama knows that she must continue to hang on
While teaching her children right from wrong
And through it all, mama's got to be strong
For mama's got to make it for her kids and for herself
Because other than the good Lord above
She really can't depend on anyone else
Yes, mama's got to make it for her kids and for herself
Mama's Got to Make It

~ ~ ~

In Due Time

If we humble ourselves under God's almighty hands
In due time everything will be all right
For He shall lift us up and help us to stand
So don't get weary and give up on life
Hold on and be strong through disappointments and strife
For if we humble ourselves under God's almighty hands
In due time everything is going to be all right
In Due Time

Come Inside   *Beverly Leonard*

The Land of Lost Hopes and Dreams

There is a land of lost hopes and dreams
Where nothing is as it really seems
A place where plans are plummeted and aspirations are lost
Where dreams are dashed and deferred
And hopes are scattered, shattered, and tossed
Where inspirations and anticipations
Are evaporated like the sweet morning dew
And into the crevices and cracks of life
High expectations plunge and fall through
Where plans and projects are left abandoned and forsaken
Where optimism and enthusiasm are agitated, jolted, and shaken
Where desires are diminished, drained, and depleted
Where self-esteems and confidences are conquered and defeated
A place where forgotten visions and goals reside
Where disappointment, despair, and frustration live side by side
A dry, dusty, and barren place is this forgotten land
Where nothing grows, but lingers in a death-like state
So lifeless, lethargic, sullen, insipid, and bland
Yet, even in this dark, dismal, and death-like place
A faint, yet flickering gleam of hope can be felt and seen
For, every now and then, someone will come along
And reclaim and resurrect a lost hope, vision, or dream
Blowing into them the spirit of life, vigor, and vitality
And that which was once forsaken becomes a reality
If you have any lost hopes and dreams that are worth fulfilling
Go to the land of lost hopes and dreams and retrieve them
And in your heart, conceive them, believe in them, and achieve them
From the land of lost hopes and dreams
Where nothing is as it really seems
The Land of Lost Hopes and Dreams

~ ~ ~

The Roadmap for Life

Our Creator lovingly left us a Roadmap behind
So that truth, wisdom, hope, and salvation we all can find
Thank you, Heavenly Father, for the Roadmap you left behind
The Roadmap for Life

Make a Plan

It is important to have a plan
For, without a plan, you're simply blowing in the wind
Being tossed to and fro and here and there
Going this way and that way, yet really going nowhere
Instead of trying to make things happen
You allow and let things happen to you
It's like sitting on the railroad tracks
And you hear the train a' coming, choo, choo
Yet, you sit there and do nothing for yourself
Knowing full well that if you fail to move
The train will roll right over you
You who are without a plan

With a plan, life becomes more focused, crystal, and clear
You can look straight ahead without dread and fear
And even though with a plan life may still try to get you down
When you have a plan, especially one in which the Lord is found
Then hope and faith are sure to abound
And upon these things you can lean, call, and depend upon
And they will lift you up, encourage you, and help make you strong
Strong enough to implement your plan and put it into action
And bring unto the Lord and to yourself great joy and satisfaction

So, if you have a plan, make sure that God is in it
And unto Him make sure you humbly present it
If you are living without a plan for your life
More than likely you are being driven like the wind
Consumed with chaos, conflict, confusion, and strife
If so, make yourself a plan today without further delay
And your life will be refreshened like the sweet morning dew
And the seeds of hope and faith
Will immediately begin to sprout and spring forth inside of you
Yes, make yourself a plan and make sure that you put God in it
And then unto the Lord, with a humble heart, submit it
Then do the things that must be done to get you where you want to go
Hey, look up ahead, what is it
It's a beautiful rainbow
Make a Plan

Be Determined

Be determined to be and do whatever it is that you want to be or do
Just as long as it brings honor and glory to the good Lord
Yes, put Him first in all that you do
And blessings from Heaven will surely rain down upon you
Be determined
Be determined to walk those long extra miles if you must
For, sometimes, life can get extra difficult, stressful, and tough
But through it all, you must remember in good times and in hard
To always call, lean, trust, and depend upon the Lord
Be determined
Be determined to complete what you begin and endure until the end
And don't give in, give up, or give out
And listen not when old satan, the deceiver comes along
To try to discourage you with fear, worry, dread, and doubt
Be determined
Yes, be determined to be and do whatever it is you want to be or do
Just as long as it brings honor and glory to the good Lord
Put Him first in all that you do
And blessings from Heaven will surely rain down upon you
Be Determined

~ ~ ~

You Can Always Go Back Home

If from the narrow path you have rambled and roamed
Please know, my beloved one, you can always go back home
For like the prodigal son who also lost his way
Your Heavenly Father anxiously awaits your return today
With open and loving arms, He is ready to receive you
For He has never stopped loving or caring about you
So, if from the narrow path you have rambled and roamed
Please know, my beloved one, you can always go back home
You Can Always Go Back Home

Who's Waiting on Whom

Sometimes we think that we're waiting on the Lord
But actually, it is the good Lord who is waiting on us
Waiting ever so patiently, for He is mighty merciful
And He has not forgotten that we came from dust
Yes, many times we think that we're waiting on the Lord
But in reality, it is the Lord who is waiting on us
Waiting ever so patiently for us to reach the next level
Of mental and spiritual enlightenment of our minds
So that true wisdom, knowledge, and discernment
And greater blessings from on high we all shall find
And yes, it says in the holy, divine, and inspired Word
That when we know not what to do or which way to turn to
We should stand still and see just what the Lord can do
But He didn't intend for us to stand still forever
For there come times in our lives when we have to move
So, are you still waiting to see what the Lord can do
Or is it the Lord who is patiently waiting on you
Who's Waiting on Whom

~ ~ ~

We Must Learn To Wait On the Lord

We must learn to wait on the Lord
And not get over-anxious and agitated when times get difficult and hard
For the Lord is never slow, languid, or late, but He's always right on time
In fact, it is time that He lovingly gives us to help develop our minds
So, let us learn to wait on the Lord
Especially when times get difficult, stressful, and hard
And let us pray for patience, which is a fruit of the Holy Spirit
A good gift from the good Lord above
Who is so merciful, kind, compassionate, and so full of grace and love
We Must Learn To Wait On the Lord

Come Inside   *Beverly Leonard*

Now March

Look forward, eyes straight ahead, now march
And don't you dare turn around and look back
Learn your lessons and learn them well
In order not to go through the same old heartaches and hell
And remember to help your sisters and brothers along life's way
Yes, you must help prevent others from stumbling and falling astray
And if you get weary and tired before your journey's end
Remember that upon the Lord you can always call, lean, trust, and depend
And unto you, renewed strength like an eagle, He will surely send
So, look forward, eyes straight ahead, now march
Now March

~ ~ ~

God Will Make A Way

God will make a way and He's always right on time
And if He doesn't come just when we want him to come
It's because He's giving us time to strengthen our minds
God will make a way and He's always right on time
God Will Make A Way

~ ~ ~

Go Through It with the Good Lord

This old world can sometimes be quite difficult and hard
So, we might as well go through it with the good Lord
For without Him to call, lean, trust, and depend upon
Our lives will be even more difficult and rock-hard
So, we might as well go through it with the good Lord
Go Through It with the Good Lord

Into The Hands of the Lord

I've come to the realization
That no matter how hard I try I just can't do it all
And that the harder I try to make things right
The harder I seem to slip, trip, stumble, and fall
So, from here on out, I'll continue to do my very best, oh, yes
But when life gets much too difficult, stressful, and hard
I shall turn it all over into the mighty hands of the good Lord
For God can make ways out when it seems there are no ways out
For He knows exactly what our lives and our living are all about
So, from here on out, I'm going to constantly call upon the Lord
Trusting in Him completely in both good times and hard
And because of my faith in His power of deliverance
I shall place all of my burdens before His holy throne
And pray that He will continue to lead, guide, and protect me
And help lift me up, fortify me, and help make me strong
And if you happen to see me in the midst of my tribulations
And you behold a sense of peace and tranquility upon my face
Please know that it's because of God's goodness, mercy, and grace
And that into the hands of the Lord all of my worries I have placed
For I've come to the realization
That no matter how hard I try I just can't do it all
And that the harder I try to make things right
The harder I seem to slip, trip, stumble, and fall
So, from here on out, I'm placing all of my burdens
Into the hands of the Lord
Into The Hands of the Lord

~ ~ ~

Don't Do It

Don't do anything today
That you will regret doing tomorrow
For such actions may cause great heartache, pain, turmoil, and sorrow
So, in order to avoid such dire consequences
Don't do anything today
That you will regret doing tomorrow
Don't Do It

Life Is . . .

Life is . . .
A song worth singing
A bell worth ringing
A poem worth penning
A prize worth winning
A story worth telling
An idea worth selling
A test worth taking
A journey worth making
A sunset worth beholding
A lump of clay worth molding
A lesson worth learning
An award worth earning
A bridge worth crossing
A ball worth tossing
A river worth swimming
A mountain worth ascending
A novel worth reading
Advice worth heeding
A sight worth seeing
A program worth attending
A message worth sending
A goal worth achieving
A truth worth believing
A dream worth pursuing
A vow worth renewing
A meal worth eating
A project worth completing
A step worth taking
A pastry worth baking
A thought worth sharing
A risk worth daring
A promise worth keeping
A mind worth reaching
A compliment worth giving
Yes, all in all, life is truly worth living
Life Is . . .

Intertwined

Mankind is like a beautiful handcrafted quilt
Lovingly designed, woven, and spun
By the Greatest Weaver of all times
Yes, created by the Most Holy One
Like a beautiful handcrafted quilt is Mankind
Perfectly interlaced
        Interlocked
                Interwoven
                      Intertwined
Such is Mankind
Intertwined

Chapter Four

Relationships: The Ins and the Outs

A Part of the Whole

A cup of ocean water
No matter how small or insignificant it may seem to be
Is still a part of the mighty and majestic deep blue sea
It is a part of the whole
And God blew into Mankind the Spirit of Life
And Mankind became a living soul
(Amen, Amen, Amen)
Therefore, the Spirit that dwells within me
Like the cup of water from the sea
Is a part of the whole
The holy and divine Spirit of God
How awesome and mind-blowing is this reality
To know that the Spirit of God resides within me
And just as the cup of ocean water shall one day return to the sea
My spirit shall one day return to the One who gave it to me
Upon the completion of my earthly journey
A Part of the Whole

~ ~ ~

The Rainbow Called Man

If all the races of Mankind
Were to stand in one straight line
The colors would blend so perfectly
Yes, it would be, oh, so divine
For one would be unable to tell
Exactly where one race ends and the next begins
For we all make up The Rainbow
The Rainbow called Man
The Rainbow Called Man

One People Under God

You say your people and I say mine
But it's time for us both to understand and realize
That we are all one people under God
For by His precious blood we all came to be
One People called the Human Family
Therefore, my people are your people
And your people are mine whether we like it or not
And we'd better start loving one another as we know we should
Before we all end up in a place that is extremely hot
One People Under God

~ ~ ~

A Mirror Poem

One Water	One People
Though we name	Though we name
The different	The different
Bodies of water	Groups of people
That cover the Earth	That live on the Earth
The oceans and the rivers	The Negroid and the Mongoloid
The lakes and the bays	And the Caucasoid
There's really one water	There's really one people
One great and massive	One great and massive people
Body of water that fell	Created in the image
To the Earth in Noah's day	And likeness of the Lord
One Water	One People

~ ~ ~

No Man Is an Island

No man is an island and no man stands alone
That's why God created woman
To help create a happy, united, and loving home
Because no man is an island and no man stands alone
No Man Is an Island

True Love Sees

True love sees no color line
For true love is truly colorblind
It sees no shades, tints, hues, or tones
For no color in true love you shall find
For true love is truly colorblind
True love sees no age
For true love began long before our earthly births
And it shall continue beyond our earthly graves
For true love sees no age
True love sees no nationalities
For true love is many races, yet only one Mankind
For we came from the same root and the same foundation
And in this sameness, great commonalities we do find
True love sees no nationalities
For though we are many, we are all one Mankind
True love sees no color, age, or nationalities
It only sees the good that is in you and me
It connects us all to the good Lord and also to one another
Joyfully proclaiming without a shadow of a doubt
That we're all true sisters and brothers
True Love Sees

~ ~ ~

We Need Each Other

Whether we choose to believe it or not
It's completely and absolutely true
You need me and I need you
For this is the way it was meant to be
Mankind living together in harmony
So, whether we choose to believe it or not
I need you and you need me
We Need Each Other

Come Inside   *Beverly Leonard*

When a Man Loves a Woman

Someone once said:
"If loving you is wrong, then I don't want to be right
If being right means being without you
I'd rather be wrong than right"
That person had a show nuff love jones
It reminds me of the first man Adam and his woman Eve
The one who was thoroughly conned, hoodwinked, and deceived
Here was his woman whom he loved with all of his might
And here was his Creator who gave him the gift of life
Adam was stuck between a rock and a very hard place
For his decision would affect the whole human race
Well, we know how the story ended
And how Adam chose his love for his woman
Over his love for the good Lord
And ever since that day when true joy and peace went away
Life on Earth has been extra difficult, stressful, and rock-hard
When a Man Loves a Woman

~ ~ ~

An Ode to Elderly Married Couples

I love to see elderly married couples who are still together
Despite many trials, tribulations, heartaches, and stormy weather
Yet, they chose to remain true to their vows made before the Lord
Through thick and through thin they both hung in
In both good times as well as when times were hard
And, oh, how it pleases and delights the Lord so
To see such love, dedication, and devotion shown here below
Thank you, dear elderly married couples
For proving that true love can indeed stand the test of time
And for setting fine standards that are good, godly, and sublime
Hats off to you for faithfully going through together
An Ode to Elderly Married Couples

Where Is the Love

Where is the love between family and kin
Where is the love between neighbors and friends
Where is the love for strangers we happen to meet
Who may very well be angels we fail to greet
Where is the love between . . .
Husbands and wives
Parents and children
Sisters and brothers
Aunts, uncles, grandparents, and cousins
Where is the love for the sick and for the elderly
Where is the love for the homeless and for the hungry
Where is the love for the animals whom we are suppose to protect
Where is the love for the Earth that we pollute and neglect
Where is the love between the nations of Mankind
Where is the love for God and for His Word that He left behind
For I've looked all around, but not a lot of love I have found
For hatred, bigotry, envy, jealousy and stupidity flourish and abound
Where is the Love

~ ~ ~

A World Without Love

A world without love is a world filled with . . .
Anxieties, apprehensions, worries, frets, frights, and fears
Headaches, heartaches, afflictions, pains, dismay, and tears
Panic, pandemonium, mayhem, mess, and madness
Suffering, sorrow, anguish, woe, wretchedness, and sadness
Selfishness, greed, bitterness, bigotry, and badness
Troubles, trials, turmoil, torment, ills, and tribulations
Competition, opposition, friction, division, and confrontations
Darkness, disaster, difficulties, defeat, ruin, and alienation
Chaos, confusion, conflict, commotion, and catastrophes
Terror, tension, violence, destruction, corruption, and calamities
Anger, angst, aggression, frustration, disagreement, and dread
Hostilities, cruelties, wars, struggles, and bloodshed
Hopelessness, hurt, desperation, depression, and misery
Disrespect, disregard, ignorance, hatred, and apathy
A World Without Love

Step Outside of Yourself

Step outside of yourself and take a good look at your life
See just **who** and **what** it is that is causing you happiness and joy
As well as what is causing you heartache, pain, stress, sorrow, and strife
Yes, step outside of yourself and take a good look at your life

Step outside of yourself and take a good look around
See just who and what it is that sends your spirit soaring high
Or sends your spirit spiraling to the cold hard ground
Yes, step outside of yourself and take a good look around

Step outside of yourself and see the place that you are in
Examine the road that got you to this point in your life
For in order to know where you're going
You must first understand where you've been
Yes, step outside of yourself and see the place that you are in

Step outside of yourself and see who the people are in your life
Are they lifters, up-builders, and encouragers
Or do they cause you nothing but trouble, turmoil, and strife
Yes, step outside of yourself and see who the people are in your life

Step outside of yourself and see what the Lord has done for you
See how He has delivered and brought you safely through
See how He has touched and blessed your life in so many ways
Yes, step outside of yourself and see what the Lord has done for you

And when you step outside of yourself to check yourself
You must be completely honest concerning what you see
For this is how we grow and how we discern and come to know
It is how we reach our self-actualization and our true destiny

And when you step outside of yourself to take a good look at your life
If you like the way your life is going, please continue on your way
But if you find that your life is full of trouble, turmoil, and strife
Then on the same destructive road you must not stay
Step Outside Of Yourself

Why We Stay

We stay in relationships for many different reasons
Some last a lifetime while others last for only a season
~
There are those who stay because of their love and devotion
For their children as well as for their mates
They hold true to their vows made before the Lord
They remain faithful and true in both good times and hard
There are those who stay because of the children
For another sad statistic they wish not to be
They put their own happiness on the back burners
In order not to split up the family
There are those who stay because of routine and habit
For they've become accustomed to a certain way of life
And in order to continue their comfortable way of living
They put up with the charades, the shams, and also the strife
There are those who stay though true love has died
Because, for their mates, they still continue to care
And they wish not to hurt, offend, or cause them pain
And for this very reason, they choose to remain
There are those who stay because they see no other way
For their self-esteem and pride have been ripped and torn into
Through ridicule, disrespect, and total neglect
They are made to feel as if there is nothing they can do
There are those who stay because the majority of their lives
Have been built around and devoted exclusively to their mates
And just the thought of trying now to make it on their own
Is frustrating and frightening, for now they think it is too late
There are those who stay because of monetary reasons
For their mates manage and control the financial strings
And to leave would be to abandon the fortune and wealth
And all the luxuries and comforts that money can bring
There are those who stay because they fear for their lives
For they are threatened by violent and abusive mates
They're afraid to go, yet they're afraid to stay
But knowing they must escape before it becomes too late
Tell me, why do you stay
Why We Stay

Before We Can Love Another

Before we can love another, we must first love ourselves
For if we fail to love ourselves first
We'll be unable and incapable of loving anyone else
And in our quest to love ourselves
We'll discover the greatest love of all times
A love so great and a love so grand
Yes, we'll discover the love that God has for Mankind
Yes, before we can love another
We must first love ourselves and also the good Lord
Because any relationship formed without these great loves
Are sure to be chaotic, difficult, strained, and rock-hard
Before We Can Love Another

~ ~ ~

It Takes Three

It takes three to make a marriage work
The man, the woman, and also the good Lord
And without these three working together in unity
The marital union will be unbalanced, difficult, and hard
Now, many have tried to make their marriage work
Without including the presence of the Lord
Only to end up with their marriages running amok
Unevenly yoked and on different marital accords
For without the Lord in the center of your marriage
Your marriage will be empty and void of many essential things
Like true dedication, devotion, heartfelt caring, and sharing
And the love, honor, and respect these essential elements bring
Without the Lord in your marriage
Your union will be filled with heartache, mistrust, and doubt
And no matter how you try to fix it or patch it up
Without the Lord in your marriage
Your marriage just won't work out
Yes, it takes three to make a marriage work
The man, the woman, and also the good Lord
And without these three working together in unity
The marital union will be unbalanced, difficult, and hard
It Takes Three

Beware Of False Faces

You can't judge books by their outside covers
Nor can you judge people by their external looks
For the exterior parts may look quite appealing
But inside may lurk real culprits, convicts, and crooks
With crooked hearts and crooked minds
Out for selfish and greedy gain
Lying and deceiving, manipulating, and scheming
Creating for others all sorts of hurts, heartaches, and pains
For these kinds of people like to put on airs
Pretending that they're someone else
Phony, fake, and fabricating
Hiding their true and treacherous real selves
They will steal the hearts of the innocent ones
For to them it is only a game
But how long can this masquerade continue
How long can their false faces remain
For how we think and how we feel
Will eventually reveal itself and come to light
Through our words, our deeds, and our actions
And it may end up in one huge and horrible fight
For truth cannot spring forth from lies and deceit
For lies have ways of reproducing and multiplying
Snowballing and smothering all that is good
For that is the very nature of lying
So, we must all become better readers
Of people as well as books
For you can't judge either one
Simply by their outside looks
Beware Of False Faces

~ ~ ~

True Friendship

True friendship must be tried and tested over and over time
To weed out the falsehoods, the deceit, the betrayals, and the lies
Yes, true friendship must be tried and tested over and over time
True Friendship

Beware of Fair-Weathered Friends

Beware of fair-weathered friends
For fair-weathered friends will forsake and betray you in the end
Now, just as long as things are going well, they hang around
But when trouble comes, fair-weathered friends just won't be found
For fair-weathered friends will pack up and move on
Because fair-weathered friendships don't last too long
So, beware of fair-weathered friends who fake and pretend
Because for you and for your welfare
Fair-weathered friends just really don't care
Beware of fair-weathered friends
For they'll forsake and betray you in the very end
Beware of Fair-Weathered Friends

~ ~ ~

You Can't Tell Everyone Your Dreams

You can't tell everyone your dreams
For everyone you tell is not going to wish you well
In fact, there will be those who shall seek
To send you and your dreams straight to hell
Remember Joseph who shared his dreams with his brothers
That one day they would bow down, honor, and serve him
Well, as far as Joseph's dreams were concerned
His brothers weren't trying to hear them
So, they sold their brother into bondage and slavery
But despite their efforts to destroy his dreams
Joseph's dreams still became reality
For whatever blessings God has in store for you
These blessings you shall surely receive
If in His Holy Word you live and believe
But in order to prevent a lot of hating on you
You must watch whom you tell your dreams to
For you can't tell everyone your dreams
For everyone you tell is not going to wish you well
If fact, there will be those who shall seek
To send you and your dreams straight to hell
You Can't Tell Everyone Your Dreams

Keep It to Yourself

Some things just don't need to be said
We need to just keep them to ourselves
For if these things are spoken and said
They, more than likely, will create and cause
Great chaos, conflict, confusion, and dread
Because some things just don't need to be said
Therefore, let us think them if we must
Then let us turn them into mere mental dust
And by-pass all the misunderstandings and the fuss
Because some things just don't need to be said
Keep It to Yourself

~ ~ ~

Our Own Medicine

A lot of good medicine to others we sometimes give
But sometimes our very own medicine we need to take
For just as taking the medicine is good for other to do
The same medicine is sometimes good for us, too
Our Own Medicine

~ ~ ~

Worry Not What People Say

Worry not what people say about you
For people will talk until they turn black and blue
But worry instead about what the Lord will say
About how you loved and lived your life on Judgment Day
Moreover, if we all would keep this point in mind
We would all get along in life superbly and just fine
Worry Not What People Say

People Are Going To Talk About You

People are going to talk about you
They're going to talk if you do
They're going to talk if you don't
They're going to talk if you will
They're going to talk if you won't
They're going to talk about this
They're going to talk about that
They're going to talk if you're skinny
They're going to talk if you're fat
They're going to talk if you're poor
They're going to talk if you're rich
They're going to talk if you're a saint
They're going to talk if you're a b----
They're going to talk about what you have
They're going to talk about what you lack
They're going to talk if you're white
They're going to talk if you're black
They're going to talk about your mama
They're going to talk about your dad
They're going to talk if you're happy
They're going to talk if you're sad
The bottom line is that people are going to talk about you
They talked about Jesus and did to Him far worse than that
So, people are going to talk about you, too, and that's a fact
So, let them talk and let their talk roll down your back
Because people are going to talk
People Are Going To Talk About You

~ ~ ~

Faultfinders

Some people try to find fault in everybody and in everything
Not realizing or caring not about the unhappiness that they bring
They're unhappy with their own lives and want others to be the same
But please don't become a victim or fall prey to the faultfinders' game
Be aware and beware of them, for unhappy souls are they
And for the faultfinders, please remember to always pray
Faultfinders

Good People

There are still some good people left in this world
Some good men, good women, and good little boys and girls
Yes, there are still some good people left in this world
And when we come across these good men, women, boys, and girls
We think: Humm, there's still some good people left in this world
Good People

~ ~ ~

Sticks and Stones

It must have been a fool who said
That sticks and stones may break our bones
But words can never hurt
For words have the power to create happiness and joy
And words also have the power these very things to destroy
For words can bring about great heartache, misery, and pain
In fact, words have been known in many situations
To cause many people to snap and go completely insane
Words have destroyed great kingdoms, kinships, and friendships
They have devastated once strong self-esteems and relationships
They have caused many tears to fall and many tears to flow
They have caused more heartache than we'll probably ever know
So, let us be ever so careful and mindful of the words that we say
For they can up-lift and enhance or wreck and ruin someone's day
Yes, sticks and stones may break our bones
But words have the power to pierce our very souls
And cause our spirit to plunge way down below
Sticks and Stones

~ ~ ~

Watch What You Say

Watch what you say
For what you say
Will come back upon you one day
For both good and for bad
So, watch what you say
Watch What You Say

Come Inside   *Beverly Leonard*

Looking For Love in All the Wrong Places

When we fail to receive the love that we really need
We may try to find it in all the wrong places
We look here and we look there trying to find love
In many different situations, circumstances, and faces

There are those who try to find love in material things
And in all the luxuries and comforts that money can bring
But money and material things bring only temporary joy
And the love of money has caused many lives to be destroyed

There are those who try to find love in mind-altering drugs
Which turn them into mindless junkies and dangerous thugs
Temporary feel-goods but crying and dying inside
For from the harsh realities of life we cannot forever hide

There are those who try to find love in other people
Depending upon another for their joy and their peace of mind
But this, too, can prove to be merely a temporary thing
For disappointment and heartache this usually brings

If true love is what you're really trying to find
A love that will last until the end of time (and beyond)
Don't look to the left or to the right
But look up instead to the Giver and the Receiver of life

For the love of the Lord is the only real and perfect thing
For true joy and peace of mind only He can bring
And if we put Him first in all that we do
Everything else will be added unto me and you

He will bless our lives with every good and perfect thing
If only to Him, in truth and in spirit, our prayers we bring
He will lift us up and out of our depressive state of mind
And in our hearts, true joy and peace of mind we all shall find

So, let us look to the Lord for perfect love
And He shall rain down blessings upon us from Heaven above
Perfect Love is Found Only In the Lord

A Low Profile

It's best to keep a low profile in these times and days
Because people are acting in the craziest and worst of ways
For they have turned from God and have fallen astray
So, it's best to keep a low profile in these times and days
Because when you style and profile and stand out in a crowd
Both the good and the bad are both checking you out
And it's because of the bad that this message has come about
And this is not to say that we should never style and profile
For it does the mind, heart, and soul good to dress up sometimes
Because when we look good, we feel good deep down inside
But because people are acting in the craziest and worst of ways
It's best to keep a low profile in these times and days
A Low Profile

~ ~ ~

Look Around You

Always be aware of your environment
Know just who and what is going on all around you
Be aware of both the seen and the unseen as well
Of those who mean you gain and good
And those who seek to bring you trouble and hell
Yes, always be aware of your environment
Look Around You

~ ~ ~

Don't Hate

When others receive blessings from on high
Don't hate and despise these blessed ones
But rejoice and be happy for them
And pray that your blessing, too, will surely come
Don't Hate

Come Inside   *Beverly Leonard*

Love Is Like a Rock

Love is like a rock
Both are natural, forceful, and strong
Bursting forth from places deep, deep within
Both shaped and formed by external forces
One by the natural elements – the winds and the waters
The other by situations and circumstances of life
The winds do blow and the waters do flow
Smoothing the jagged edges of the rocks away
And the struggles of life can sometimes work like glue
Bonding the love and the commitment made by the two
But too much pressure and too much stress
Can cause both to crumble and depart
The once strong rock will turn into dust
And true love will no longer be found in the heart
So, be careful how you treat the ones you love
Or, like dust, **poof**, it will be gone
Love Is Like a Rock

~ ~ ~

Didn't I Tell You

Fool . . . Didn't I tell you that love is like a rock
That if you continue to misuse and abuse it
Then, like dust, **poof**, it will be gone
Didn't I tell you that one day you'd wake up
Sad, lonely, broken-down, depressed, and so all alone
And it is impossible to restore true love ever again
For like a trodden and beaten-down rock
True love has crumbled and turned to sand
Now, since you had to go and blow your good thing
You must now face the consequences
That your negative and foolish actions bring
Book it under hard lessons of life, hard-knocks, and strife
And next time, if you're blessed with a next time
You just might get it right
Didn't I Tell You

Little Things Mean a Lot

Sometimes we forget about the little things
And therefore, we fail to receive the pleasure and the happiness
That these little things bring
Little things like . . .
A soothing backrub after a hard day's work
A passionate kiss
A soft caress
A gentle touch that means so very much
A walk in the park hand in hand
Enjoying the soothing music of a jazz band
A nice romantic ride along the countryside
A cozy picnic in the park
Watching the sunset just before dark
An evening out just the two
A whisper that says, "I love you"
A candlelit dinner with bubbly delight
A close-up snuggle in the middle of the night
A compliment for something either said or done
Open arms in which to freely run
Listening ears that truly hear
A warm embrace that helps to ease the fears
Flowers received for no particular reason
For love stays in bloom throughout the four seasons
So, let us not forget about the little things
In order to enjoy the pleasures and happiness that they bring
For these little things mean a lot
For they keep love strong and running red-hot
Little Things Mean a Lot

~ ~ ~

Don't Forget the Little Things

Don't forget the little things and going those extra miles
Because it's the little things that make the big things worthwhile
Don't Forget the Little Things

Both Sides of the Door

If it's not right on the other side of the bedroom door
Don't expect it to be right on the inside
In fact, don't expect or anticipate anything more
For what happens outside of the bedroom door
Directly affects what will happen on the inside
And from this fact of reality we cannot run or hide
If there is a lack of communication on the outside
There will be no caring conversations on the inside
If there is no caring and sharing shown on the outside
There will only be selfish acts of satisfaction on the inside
If, on the outside, there are no hugs, warm caresses, and kisses
Then on the inside, these things will also be missing
If passion and emotion are lacking on the outside
Don't expect to find them anywhere on the inside
If the fire and the flames are not burning on the outside
Then frigid, cold, and chilly it will be on the inside
Therefore, if you desire the flames and the fire
The communication and the conversation
The caring and the heart-felt sharing
The gentle hugs, kisses, caresses, and feelings of love
The heated passions and fervent emotions
The strong sense of caring, dedication, and devotion
Then make sure that these things are present and evident
On the other side of the bedroom door
For if it's not right on the other side
Don't expect the inside to be anything more
Both Sides of the Door

~ ~ ~

The First Stone

The first stone continues to sit on the ground
For no one without sin on the Earth can be found
So, the first stone continues to sit on the ground
The First Stone

I'm Only Human

I'm only human
What more do you expect
I have human desires and human needs
Cut my skin and I'm sure to bruise and bleed
For, I'm only human
So, don't expect anything more
I'll try hard to do my best, but as I said before
I'm only human
And as hard as I try to do my best
I'm sure to fail some of life's trials and tests
And guess what, you will fail sometimes, too
Because you're only human
You'll also bleed and bruise if someone were to cut you
So, we're both only human
Neither of us are perfect or without a single flaw
That's why we must always remember
That love is the key and the sum of the law
For not one, no not one, can be found without one flaw
And let us be happy to be human beings
For we were created from the divine image of the good Lord
And He understands our strengths and also our weaknesses
He knows that our living can sometimes get mighty hard
And because He has not forgotten that we came from dust
He is mighty merciful and kind, and from our sins, He forgives us
And we, too, must learn to forgive one another
And accept each other as true sisters and brothers
For we are all only human
We're Only Human

~ ~ ~

Nobody's Perfect

Nobody's perfect neither you nor I
And perfect we will never be on this side
No matter what we do or how hard we try
Because nobody's perfect neither you nor I
Nobody's Perfect

The Givers and the Takers

In this world, there are the Givers and the Takers
~
The givers are those who are always giving
They give their time, their talents, their energy, and their love
The givers do all they can to help up-lift their fellow man
All of which draws the givers closer to the Lord above
The givers of this world are compassionate, faithful, and true
They are kind, considerate, and loving through and through
You shall recognize the givers by their fruits
~
The takers are those who are always taking
Yet, hardly ever give anything back in return
They are always looking for ways to lift themselves
For they care little or nothing about the lives of anyone else
They are self-centered and full of selfish greed
They want no one but themselves to prosper, excel, and succeed
They're not to be trusted, for in them, trust cannot be found
They are the ones who hate to see another make it
They are the ones who pull you down to the cold, hard ground
So, be aware and beware of the takers
You shall recognize them by their fruits
The Givers and the Takers

~ ~ ~

Move On

When those around you fail to believe in you
They will lack faith in what you think, say, and do
(Like they did Jesus in His hometown)
And because of their lack of faith
A lack of miracles and blessings will be in this place
And sometimes it may be best to just move on
Even from your familiar, yet faithless home
Yes, sometimes it may be best to just move on
Move On

Just Because You Can

Just because you can doesn't mean that you should
Just because you think it's right doesn't make it all good
For your actions and your reactions affect the lives of others
Not only strangers that you meet, but also your sisters and brothers
Just because you were born with a silver spoon
And you live in luxuries beyond compare
Doesn't mean that you should belittle those less fortunate
But you should lift them up instead
Then maybe your life the Lord shall spare
Just because you are beautiful and possess great charm
And can catch every man's wandering and roving eye
Doesn't mean you should lower yourself or your standards
Or for these very reasons you could certainly die
Just because you are handsome and can play the ladies
And treat them with great contempt and disrespect
Doesn't mean that you should offend, misuse, or abuse them
For these very actions, you, the Lord will certainly reject
Remember, Jesus was tempted by the devil himself
After fasting forty days and forty nights
Yes, He could have turned the stones into bread
And feasted in utmost ecstasy and delight
He was then taken to the Holy City
Where He stood on the highest peak
And, yes, He could have thrown Himself right down
And landed flat upon His feet
Finally, to the mountaintop the Lord was taken
And shown the great kingdoms of the world
And, yes, He could have bowed down before the evil one
But He knew that into the flames of hell
This manslayer would soon be hurled
So, just because you can doesn't mean that you should
Just because you think it's right doesn't make it all good
Hold on to your integrity and you'll hold on to life
Before you do anything just because you can
You'd better always think twice
Just Because You Can

Come Inside   *Beverly Leonard*

How Can You Forget So Easily

You witnessed your father beating your mother
And it pained your heart deep down inside
You tried to shut the hurt and pain away
But from the hurt and pain you could not run or hide
Oh, how you wished you could have helped your mom
Against the brutal attacks of your out-of-control dad
For his abusive actions against your dear and loving mother
Left you heartbroken, shattered, torn, angry, and sad

Now, many years have passed, but the cycle of abuse continues to last
For you have become the very same monster just like your dad
You have taken on his same destructive behaviors and ways
You are now making someone else's life miserable and sad
Tell me, how can you repeat such hostile and hurtful actions
How can you dare lift your hand to strike and abuse another
How can you forget so easily the pain and the hurt
And all of the suffering that your father caused your mother

Have you forgotten the hurt and the pain you felt back then
Have you forgotten the heartache it caused you deep within
Have you forgotten how, from the pain, you tried to hide
Have you forgotten the anger and the rage you felt inside

You **must** wake up now and face your demons from the past
You must not allow this vicious cycle to continue to last
For now your children are looking and listening
At everything that you say and do
And if you fail to break this destructive cycle
More than likely, they will become victims and abusers, too

You must break this deadly cycle now, for it's not right, nor is it okay
And remember, the Lord is coming soon to set matters straight
And if you continue your violent and destructive ways
You'll have nothing but hell and retribution to pay
I'm praying that this viscous cycle you shall break
Do it now before it is too late
How Can You Forget So Easily

How Can You

How can you dare say that you love me
Then you turn around
And you physically, mentally, verbally, and emotionally
Misuse and abuse me
How can you dare say that you love me
How can you
How can you hold me in your arms in the middle of the night
Then with the same hands, you reach out to strike me
Filling my heart with great pain, heartache, and fright
How can you
How can you whisper sweet nothings in my ear
Then with the same mouth, you verbally abuse me
Filling my mind with great dread, terror, and fear
How can you
How can you be so pleasant and enchanting one moment
Then the next moment you're cold as ice
A **Jerky**ll and Hyde sort of insanity
One moment you're rude, then the next moment you're nice
How can you
Well, if this is true love, please count me out
For it seems that you know nothing
Of what true love is all about
But I cannot continue to live my life this way
Walking on eggshells just to please you
I'm tired of all the sadness, the stress, and the madness
I'm tired of all the hell that you put me through
I'm sorry that you missed that something special
Whatever it was that caused great sorrow in your life
And I pray that God will heal you and deliver you
And free you from your sadness, your mental pain, and strife
But if I continue on in this explosive and volatile relationship
Your negative spirit shall consume and destroy my very soul
So, I pray that God will lead, guide, and deliver me
From the grips of your consuming and controlling hold
How can you dare say that you love me
When you fail to love yourself
How Can You

It's Not Love

It's not love when he beats you and abuses you
It's not love when he falsely blames and accuses you
It's not love when he curses you out
It's not love when he rants, raves, and shouts
It's not love when he pushes, pulls, and shoves
No matter what he tells you, my sister
It's not love
It's not love when he belittles you in front of his friends
It's not love when he won't let you visit
Or talk to your family, friends, and kin
It's not love when you must jump every time he calls
It's not love when he knocks you into the walls
No matter what he tells you, my sister
It's not love
It's not love when he controls and dominates your entire life
It's not love when he causes you
Lots of heartache, pain, suffering, and strife
It's not love when he threatens to beat you black and blue
It's not love when he turns it all around
Then blames his destructive behaviors on you
No matter what he tells you, my sister
It's not love
It's not love when he begs you to forgive him
Then promises never to do it again
It's not love and it sure as hell doesn't make him a real man
It's not love just because he sends you flowers
That will eventually wilt and die
It's not love, my sister, but one sick and demented lie
No matter what he tells you, my sister
It's not love
Wake up, my sister, from this nightmarish hell that you're in
And reclaim your once-strong self-esteem, dignity, and pride
For no longer from reality can you continue to run and hide
You must free yourself from this ticking time-bomb lout
For it's only a matter of time before your time runs out
Remember, no matter what he tells you, my sister
It's not love
It's Not Love

What Love Is

Love suffers long
Love is kind
Love does not envy
Love does not parade itself
Love is not puffed up
Love does not behave rudely
Love does not seek its own
Love is not provoked
Love thinks no evil
Love does not rejoice in iniquity
Love rejoices in truth
Love bears all things
Love believes all things
Love hopes all things
Love endures all things
Love never fails
What Love Is

1 Corinthians 13:4-8

~ ~ ~

Knuckle Sandwiches

Knuckle sandwiches don't taste good at all
Especially when they knock you down and make you fall
In fact, nothing good comes from sandwiches such as these
Even when followed by, "Baby, I'm sorry, forgive me please"
For knuckle sandwiches have been known
To cause great pain, suffering, sorrow, and even death
As if the lives of those who digest them are of very little worth
So, if someone tries to serve you knuckle sandwiches
Please don't accept or take them, for if you do
The perpetrators will continue to serve them to you
And from those who serve these types of sandwiches
From them you must flee and run like hell
And to others, this message you, too, must tell
Knuckle Sandwiches

He'll Hit You Again

If he hits you one time
More than likely, he'll hit you again
As if hitting you is going to make him a big, big man
Yes, if he hits you one time, he'll hit you again and again
And if he says that he's sorry (which he is)
And promises to never hit you again
Don't believe the hype, my sister, my daughter, my niece, my friend
Because if he hits you one time
More than likely, he'll hit you again
He'll Hit You Again

~ ~ ~

Keep Your Hands to Yourself

Who do you think you are
That it's okay for you to put your hands on someone else
What gives you the right to cause hurt and harm to another
Nothing does, so keep your hands to yourself
Keep Your Hands to Yourself

~ ~ ~

Move On

If you can't get along
Don't get it on
Instead, move on
Move On

~ ~ ~

Behind Closed Doors

You never know what goes on behind closed doors
Whether the gentle sheep sleeps peacefully
Or whether the angry lion rages and roars
You never know what goes on behind closed doors
Behind Closed Doors

It's not Okay

It's not okay to hate, hurt, and harm one another
For, through God's blood, we're all true sisters and brothers
It's not okay to lie, steal, kill, covet, and cheat
Or, for these very reasons, sinners shall feel the heat
It's not okay to sleep around
So, get off your back and plant your feet on solid ground
It's not okay to have children outside of a loving home
For a strong family base helps them feel that they belong
It's not okay to have children and then rear and raise them not
For failure to do so only sets them up for a place that is hot
It's not okay to do and say ugly things in front of the kids
For this only confuses them more and makes them hit the skids
It's not okay for children to treat their parents with disrespect
Or a short life upon the Earth is what they should expect
It's not okay to be mean-spirited, impolite, crude, and rude
Walking around with a mean, nasty, and negative attitude
It's not okay to mistreat and hurt the feelings of others
Instead, we should lift, love, inspire, and encourage one another
It's not okay to do the very things the Lord rejects
And if we fail to change our evil and destructive ways
Then death and destruction is what we should expect
Because it's not okay
It's Not Okay

~ ~ ~

A Look at Your Life

If he/she pulls your good spirits down
And causes your blood pressure to rise
Then it's time to take a serious look at your life
Or your life and your living shall continue to be consumed
With heartaches, stresses, strains, and strife
A Look at Your Life

A Change Of Heart

You can't continue to treat someone bad
And possibly think that you'll have what you've always had
You can't use, misuse, abuse, and neglect them
You can't hurt, harm, mistreat, or show them disrespect
Or a change of heart is what you should expect

You see, I told you before that love is like a rock
I told you about the pros and cons of the pressures of life
I told you that too much pressure causes ruin and destruction
Causing love to fly like dust and ash during a volcanic eruption
And like a rock that has crumbled and turned into dust
A heart that has been broken, shattered, and maimed
Will never again be quite the same

So, once again, I say to all the women and men
And to all the young people who profess to love another
Learn this lesson of love and from it never depart
Or there shall continue to be broken relationships
And many sad and shattered hearts
Therefore, in order to prevent broken hearts from happening
Let us not misuse, abuse, hurt, mistreat, disrespect, and neglect
Or shattered dreams and change of hearts are what we should expect

And if you fail to heed these words once again
You are a fool in your very own right
But sooner or later these lessons you'll learn
But until that time comes, you'll live a sad and mixed-up life
For love has nothing to do with the things mentioned above
For love is pure and love is true
Love is not something that rants, raves, and shouts
And constantly beats the hell out of you
Whether physically, spiritually, emotionally
Verbally, or socially, you can't treat somebody bad
And possibly think you'll have what you've always had
You can't use, misuse, abuse, and neglect
You can't hurt, harm, mistreat, or show disrespect
Or a change of heart is what you should expect
A Change Of Heart

When Love Is Gone

When love is gone, it's best to move on
For what's the use of merely hanging on when love is gone
For, when love leaves the heart
Many essential elements soon follow and depart
Like caring and sharing for and with one another
As well as tenderness, compassion, dedication, and devotion
You don't talk anymore like you use to do
Which causes all kinds of chaos, conflict, and commotion
For, when you don't love the one that you're with
You're not really living, but you're merely existing
Such a sad way to live and even a sadder way to die
So sad it makes the angels in Heaven weep, wail, and cry
When true love is gone, it's best to move on
For what's the use of merely hanging on
When Love Is Gone

~ ~ ~

Change Yourself

You'll probably be unable to change that other person
No matter how hard you might try
You'll do this and you'll do that trying to make things right
Only to possibly end up in one huge and explosive fight
And chances are you'll be the one
Who will feel the pain and bare the scars
For, real change begins deep within
And without a desire to change one's self
Their hearts you will never ever win
So, change yourself and get on with your life
Continue not in the same old cycle of heartache and strife
Love yourself, free yourself, be yourself
Change Yourself

Come Inside   *Beverly Leonard*

To The Lonely Hearts

Though many surround us we can still feel so alone
With no one to talk to, to love, hug, and caress us
With no one to truly call our very own
Wishing that someone special would come our way
And in our hearts we wish that these special someones
Would forever in our hearts and in our lives forever stay
For we were not created to live in solitary and be all alone
That's why God created woman, so that man wouldn't be on his own
But life is full of many ups and downs, hang ups, and turn arounds
And through it all, there are many lessons that we all must learn
Through our trials and our tribulations we all must discern
And the main lessons to be learned in the valley called loneliness
Is to be patient, to wait on the Lord, and to all the time pray
That, in due time, He will send someone special our way
And though we may get lonely sometimes
We are never truly alone
For the Lord is with us each and every day
To The Lonely Hearts

~ ~ ~

You Will Smile Again

If the troubles of this old world are weighing you down
If sadness and sorrows have you burdened and bound
If the storms of life rant and rage all around
If it feels like you're standing on sinking ground
If situations and circumstances of life
Have turned your smile into a frown
Please know, my beloved one, you will smile again
Because, thank God, trouble doesn't last always
Which means that sooner or later there will be brighter days
If you just hold on through the turbulent storms and be strong
The winds and rains will cease and the dark clouds will move on
If through the storms of life you endure and hold on
You will smile again
You Will Smile Again

Somebody's Child

Somebody's child has lost their way
Somebody's child has fallen astray
Somebody's child is having a really bad day
Somebody's child is hurting today
Somebody's child is lonely and sad
Somebody's child is misbehaving and acting bad
Somebody's child is filled with great frights and fears
Somebody's child is crying a long river of tears
Somebody's child is in a state of disillusion and despair
Somebody's child feels as if no one really cares
Somebody's child has a shattered and broken heart
Somebody's child needs a brand new start
Somebody's child is far away from home
Somebody's child weeps, wails, laments, and moans
Somebody's child is sleeping in the streets
Somebody's child doesn't have enough food to eat
Somebody's child is begging on the side of the road
Somebody's child is carrying a hard and heavy load
Somebody's child is trying hard to stand
Somebody's child needs a helping hand
Somebody's child is finding it hard to cope
Somebody's child is losing or have lost all hope
Somebody's child is frustrated and confused
Somebody's child has been abandoned and abused
Somebody's child is hooked on mind-altering drugs
Somebody's child is acting like a low-down dirty thug
Somebody's child is living in sin
Somebody's child just can't seem to win
Somebody's child is incarcerated and locked away
Somebody's child doubts that they'll see a brighter day
Somebody's child is consumed with worry and doubt
Somebody's child is in pain and is stressing out
Somebody's child has lost their self-confidence
Somebody's child needs warm words of encouragement
Somebody's child is having it really, really hard
Somebody's child needs to hear the Word of the Lord
Somebody's child wants to come back home
Somebody's child is tired of being all alone

Somebody's child has lost their will to live
Somebody's child needs to know that God loves them still
Yes, this world is filled with somebody's children
They are both you and me and all of humanity
So, let's show each other love, compassion, and mercy
For, we are all somebody's child
Somebody's Child

~ ~ ~

A Brighter Day Is Coming

Though today your life may seem dreary, blurry, and bleak
As if life is trying its best to knock you completely off your feet
Hold on and be strong, for a brighter day is coming your way
And true joy and peace of mind you shall surely find one day
But while you are down in the valleys and in the vales of life
Learn your lessons well through your toils, troubles, and strife
And remember to always call upon the good Lord
For He has the power to strengthen and deliver you
Through times that are difficult, stressful, and rock-hard
So, when you're down in the valleys and in the vales of life
Hold on and be strong, for a brighter day is coming your way
A Brighter Day Is Coming

~ ~ ~

A Lasting Relationship

As we live our lives upon the Earth
Many relationships with others we are sure to form
But the most important relationship that we can ever build
Is with our Heavenly Father through his only begotten Son
For many will come into our lives and many shall surly go away
But the relationship that we form with the Lord shall forever stay
So, let us make sure that our relationship with God is firmly in tack
So that there will be no questions about it when Jesus comes back
If you've already formed a close relationship with the good Lord
Continue to build upon it with each and every passing day
If you have not formed a relationship with the Lord
Then do it now without further delay
A Lasting Relationship

Come Inside   *Beverly Leonard*

Sons are a heritage from the Lord
Children a reward from Him
Like arrows in the hands of a warrior
Are sons born in one's youth.
Blessed is the man whose quiver is full of them.

Psalm 127: 3-8

Chapter Five
Just Look to the Children

Come Inside   *Beverly Leonard*

A Voice for the Children

I am a voice for the children
For the children who are crying in the wilderness
For the children who can't find peace, joy, and happiness
For the children whose spirit can't find rest
For the children who try hard, but fail nearly every test
For the children who live in sad and broken homes
For the children who have no place to call their very own
For the children who feel that they don't belong
For the children who are lost and are a long way from home
For the children who seek righteousness but find only wrong
For the children who are left by themselves and are all alone
For the children who are abandoned, forsaken, and abused
For the children who are mistreated, deceived, and falsely accused
For the children who are bewildered, perplexed, and confused
For the children who go to bed without enough food to eat
For the children who weep and cry themselves to sleep
For the children who hunger for love, attention, and affection
For the children who lack guidance, supervision, and protection
For the children who walk the streets in the middle of the night
For the children who are filled with terror, dread, fear, and fright
For the children who are struggling and have lost their way
For the children who, from the narrow path, have fallen astray
For the children who have no one to encourage and believe in them
For the children whose future looks dark, gloomy, blight, and dim
For the children who are filled with sadness, grief, and sorrow
For the children who have little or no hope for a better tomorrow
Yes, I am a voice for the children
Now, may my voice for the children be heard both far and near
To help save the lives of our children who are so precious and dear
I am a voice for the children
A Voice for the Children

~ ~ ~

"Let the little children come to Me, and do not forbid them; for of such is the kingdom of God. Assuredly, I say to you, whoever does not receive the kingdom of God as a little child will by no means enter it."

Mark 10:12-15

Just Look to the Children

Just look to the children
Before they are misguided and misled
Just look to the children
Before on bigotry, hatred, and racism they are ill fed
Just look to the children
Observe how, with one another, they get along so well
Behold how they cooperate and exemplify true love in action
Before they're drenched in the bitter and twisted lies from hell
Just look to the children
Notice how they share and care for each other
See how they come together in unity and camaraderie
Before they are taught to hate and despise one another
Just look to the children
Listen to their heartfelt and sincere conversations
Detect their smiling faces all aglow
Listen to their lively laughter and their joyful jubilation
Just look to the children
And you shall see just how life really should be, ideally
For love is a natural and inherent kind of thing
And without love, there is division, disparity, and misery
Just look to the children of the world
Yes, look to our precious little boys and darling little girls
Look to the children before they are misguided and misled
Just look to the children
Before on bigotry, hatred, and racism they are ill fed
Just Look to the Children

~ ~ ~

Oh, Listen to the Children

Oh, listen to the children
For the children have much to say
So, listen with discerning ears to the children
Yes, listen to the children today
Oh, Listen to the Children

All Children Really Want

All children really want is a loving and happy home
To feel safe and secure and to feel that they belong
With two loving parents who really love one another
A strong and supportive father and a loving and nurturing mother
Who, together, will teach, lead, discipline, train, and guide
Who, together, will nourish, nurture, support, and provide
Yes, all children really want is a loving and happy home
To feel safe and secure and to feel that they belong
All Children Really Want

~ ~ ~

We Cannot Blame the Kids

We cannot blame the kids for hitting the skids
If we fail to rear, raise, discipline, and train them well
Yes, if we fall short on our parental and guardian duties
We should expect disrespect, heartache, hurt, and hell
We **must** do better concerning the rearing of our kids
Or our kids will surely run amok and hit the skids
We Cannot Blame the Kids

~ ~ ~

Children Can't Wait

Children can't wait for their parents to grow up
For children need their parents to be parents right from the very start
To set strong, solid, and firm foundations
That will help them to become well balanced, happy, and smart
So, parents, please be parents to your children right from the very start
Please don't wait until it's too late
Because our dear and precious children just can't wait
Children Can't Wait

Children, Don't Grow Up Too Fast

Children, don't grow up too fast
But be children just as long as you possibly can
Enjoy the basic freedom that comes with being children
And don't be in a rush to become a woman or a man
Because being grown-up isn't all that it's cracked up to be
For with it comes great stress, strain, and responsibility
And if you are blessed to be blessed to be children, be thankful
For there are many children around the world
Who are unfairly stressed, pressed, and burdened down
With too many adult responsibilities on their shoulders
That level and straddle them to the cold, hard ground
So, children, don't grow up too fast
But be children just as long as your childhood lasts
And when your childhood is over and men and women you shall be
Be prepared to deal with the stress, the strain, and the responsibility
Children, Don't Grow Up Too Fast

~ ~ ~

In The Days of Your Youth

Children, remember your Heavenly Father in the days of your youth
For this is what the scriptures do say
That you should remember your Heavenly Father
And He will lead you and guide you along the way
But, in order to remember Him, you must first come to know Him
And when you come to know of His great love for you
You will always remember and adore Him forevermore
In The Days of Your Youth

~ ~ ~

Speak, Oh, Children, Speak

Speak, oh, children, speak
For it is your time to tell the world what's on your mind
Speak, Oh, Children, Speak

From The Mouth of a Child

Please stop, look, and listen to me world
For I am the voice of every little boy and every little girl
Crying out in a loud and desperate plea
Wishing the world would stop, look, and listen to me
For the voice of every child around the world says
Lead me, nurture me, and guide me along life's way
Show me true love and understanding each and every day
Please feed me and clothe me
And provide me with a safe and loving home
Let me know that you will always be there for me
And promise me you will never leave me alone
When I fall short of perfection
Please don't criticize or look down upon me
But lift me up and show me the proper way
And help me to be the very best that I can be
Please help me to grow strong in every way
Physically, mentally, and spiritually, this I pray
Show me through your fine examples
How to live a good and up-right life
So that I may avoid unnecessary pain, suffering, and strife
Teach me the importance of love, honor, and respect
For God, myself, and also for others
Let's stop the violence and increase the peace
After all, we're all true sisters and brothers
And let's stop destroying our beautiful world
With all sorts of deadly and dangerous pollutions
Let's come together now to solve our problems
And create and maintain workable solutions
And never, no, no, no, never let a day go by
Without sharing kind words, kisses, and hugs
And that which we ask for, we'll gladly return
And that which we ask for is simply your love
So, please stop, look, and listen to me world
For I am the voice of every little boy and every little girl
Crying out in a loud and desperate plea
Wishing the world would stop, look, and listen to me
From The Mouth of a Child

Come Inside   *Beverly Leonard*

Children and Spring Flowers

Children are like beautiful spring flowers
That bloom and grow in the springtime
Created in the perfect image of the Most Holy
Who lovingly created all Mankind
Yes, children are like beautiful spring flowers
That bloom and grow in the springtime
Planted in the blessed wombs of Womankind
To carry, to nurture, and to bring into this world
Precious little boys and darling little girls
For children are indeed true gifts from Heaven above
Gifts intended to be properly reared, raised, and trained
Gifts intended to be properly cared for, disciplined, and loved
And we, as parents and guardians of our precious little ones
Our dear and darling daughters and our adorable sons
Are given this great charge and grand commission by the Lord
So, we must not leave this great responsibility
Which comes with great accountability simply to chance
Or like wildflowers and weeds our children will sadly grow
And a chance to live happy, healthy, and productive lives
Our precious children will never come to experience and know
Instead, they will be tossed and scattered
With their hopes and dreams lost, deferred, and shattered
No, we must not let our precious children grow up this way
We must lead them and guide them along life's way
So that from the narrow path our precious children will not stray
We must do right by our children each and every day
So, let us rear, raise, and train our children well
Let us care for, discipline, and love them, too
Much more than these words can possibly tell
Then, like the beautiful spring flowers
That bloom and grow in the springtime
Our children will flourish, prosper, thrive and excel
Like the beautiful spring flowers that grow so well
Children and Spring Flowers

Come Inside   *Beverly Leonard*

Seize Opportune Moments

We must seize opportune moments
To teach our children and train them well
For great harm will come if left undone
And everything else is sure to falter and fail

We must seize opportune moments
When they come along in life
To help prevent unnecessary pain and suffering
To help prevent unnecessary sadness, heartache, and strife

We must seize opportune moments
To teach our children right from wrong
Or our children will live their lives steeped in sin
And chances are they won't live too long

We must seize opportune moments
To model that which we wish to instill
Like love, honor, respect, and good manners
For these are fine characters we wish to build

For, if we fail to teach our children well
And leave it into the hands of fate
Or into the hands of the preachers and the teachers
There's a real possibility that by then it will be too late

For children form many ideas and opinions at a very early age
So, we cannot wait until it's too late
Or, by then, they will be in another stage
Then you won't be able to tell them this, that, or the other
And you can bet they'll have no respect
For God, life, themselves, their fathers, or their mothers

And we must not only seize opportune moments
But we must take time and make time each and every day
To help build and strengthen strong morals and values
For this is the only way
Parents, please teach and train your children well
And remember, parents, there is a Heaven and there is a Hell
Seize Opportune Moments

To Think and To Dream

We must teach our children to think and to dream
For, a world without thinkers and dreamers is no world at all
For the thinkers and the dreamers of the world
Are our links to the future
And it has been said by many, many times before
That our children are our future
And that without our children there shall be no tomorrow
Only a world filled with death, doom, chaos, and sorrow
And if the children are indeed our links to the future
And I believe within my heart that this is so
Then we must teach them, train them, lead, guide, and guard them
We must nurture and encourage them as they live, learn, and grow
We must teach them through our fine examples
Through the lives that we ourselves lead
Not simply by our words alone, but through our positive actions
If we want our children and our future to excel and succeed
Therefore, we must teach our children to think and to dream
But we must be thinkers and dreamers, as well
For, if we fall short or fail to reach this essential mark
Then Humanity and Mankind are destined to collapse and fail
So, let us all be thinkers and dreamers
Let us all help to create positive solutions for a better world
And let us pass these precious gifts on to our little ones
Yes, let us pass them on to every little boy and girl
So, here's to a bright and glorious future
Here's to our children
Let us teach our children to think and to dream
To Think and To Dream

~ ~ ~

Think Big

Think big and not small
Believe that you will soar and excel and not stumble and fall
Think big and not small
Think Big

If You See My Children

With my children I will not always be
So, if along life's highways and bi-ways
My children you happen to see
Please, oh, please do these things for me
If indeed the need for these things be
If you see my children in danger or in harm's way
Please try to shield them and protect them, this I pray
If you see my children down and out and in need of a helping hand
Please lift them up and help my children to stand
If you see my children and they're hungry and tired
Please give them a bite to eat and a safe place to sleep
If you see my children and they're acting in a negative way
Please pull them to the side and redirect them without delay
If you see my children and their spirits are weary and weak
Please encourage them and encourage them the Lord to seek
And even if my children you don't happen to see
Please pray for my children and for my family
And these things I will do for you
If I see your children along life's way
And even if I don't happen to see them
For your children and for your family I will pray
If You See My Children

~ ~ ~

You Can Never Tell

You can never tell just what a child will become in life
Whether he or she will turn out badly
Or whether they will do something great to help all humanity
Just because he or she is a little bit slower than the rest
Misbehaves, disobeys, and fails nearly every test
Or fills your life with worry, heartache, stress, and strife
Doesn't necessary mean they won't be successful in life
So, please don't label a child, for you can never tell
Whether they will fail in life, or in life, soar and excel
You Can Never Tell

Someone Taught Us

Someone taught us many things along the way
That helped us become the people that we are today
Someone taught us the difference between right and wrong
Someone taught us to be diligent, steadfast, determined, and strong
Someone taught us to obey the rules and be good
Someone taught us to speak and act as we know we should
Someone taught us good manners, morals, and good values, as well
Someone taught us that if we put our minds to it we will excel
Someone taught us the importance of getting a good education
Someone taught us the value of hard word and dedication
Someone taught us to listen, focus, and to do our very best
Someone taught us to prepare and strive hard on each and every test
Someone taught us that in ourselves we must always believe
Someone taught us to hold fast to our visions, goals, and dreams
Someone taught us that there is nothing in life that we cannot achieve
Someone taught us that it's more a blessing to give than to receive
Someone taught us that where there's a will there is a way
Someone taught us that on the narrow path we should strive to stay
Someone taught us to respect and cherish our elderly
Someone taught us the importance of freedom, justice, and liberty
Someone taught us to share what we have with others
Someone taught us to respect and honor our fathers and mothers
Someone taught us The Word of the Lord
Someone taught us that He is with us in both good times and hard
Someone taught us that for our neighbors we should love and care
Someone taught us the power of prayer
And we are here today
Because someone took time out to teach us a better way
We were their future back then
Just as our children are our future today
And it is our obligation to return the blessings
And to show our children a better way
So, let us teach our children and teach them well
So that they, too, will prosper, thrive, soar, and excel
Because someone taught us
Someone Taught Us

You Must Return the Blessings

Maybe there were a few special people in your life
Who helped and guided you along life's way
And because they showed true interest and concern for you
From the straight and narrow path you did not stray
Maybe someone offered kind words of encouragement
Which boosted your self-esteem and increased your confidence
Maybe someone said something that lifted your spirits high
Maybe someone inspired you to do your very best
Which motivated you to just go ahead and try
Maybe there was someone who made sure that you were fed
That your clothes were clean and your homework done
And that your prayers to the good Lord were said
Maybe someone took time out of their busy day
Just to sit and listen to what you had to say
Maybe they served as positive role models in your life
Teaching and training you in an up-right way
Maybe it was a hug, a gentle touch, or a genuine smile
That made you want to walk those extra miles
But whatever it was that was said or done
You should be thankful for those special "someones"
And now that you've made it to this point in your life
Because there were those who truly cared for you
It is only right that you return the blessings
And help others as they struggle to make it on through
For you must return the blessing
You Must Return the Blessings

~ ~ ~

The Way Blessings Go

God blesses me, then I bless you, then you bless her
Then she blesses him, and then he blesses them
Then we all bless God from whom all blessings flow
And that's the way blessings go
The Way Blessings Go

Come Inside *Beverly Leonard*

What Are We Showing Our Children

If we show our children bitterness, anger, fear, and rage
Our children will grow up angry, unhappy, lost, and afraid

If we show our children contempt, dishonor, and disrespect
Disrespectful and shameless children is what we should expect

If we show our children ignorance, idiocy, and imbecility
Then illiterate children, teens, and adults they shall grow up to be

If we show our children laziness, idleness, and unproductivity
Then poor, pathetic, and impoverished beggars they shall be

If we show our children a lack of self-esteem, dignity, and pride
Our children will lack these essential elements deep down inside

If we show our children a lack of faith and honor for the Lord
Our children will lack hope and their living will be extremely hard

However...

If we show our children true love, dedication, and caring
Then our children will be full of love, compassion, and sharing

If we show our children kindness, thoughtfulness, and concern
Then respect and reverence from our children we shall earn

If we show our children love for literacy and learning
Our children's thirst for knowledge shall forever continue burning

If we show our children perseverance and determination
Then our children will reach their goals without hesitation

If we show our children that in ourselves we believe
There will be nothing that our children cannot accomplish and achieve

If we show our children strong faith in the Lord
Our children will stand firm in the faith in good times and hard

Therefore, we must be careful what we show our precious children
For our actions and our reactions
Greatly affect the actions and reactions of our children
What Are We Showing Our Children

What Are Poor Parents to Do

Our world is filled with many marvels and wonders
With so many fascinating places to go and things to see and do
And we wish that we could share these things with our children
But, tell me, what are poor parents to do
We wish we could travel to exotic and faraway places
Like Africa, Asia, and Europe just to name a few
We'd camp out in the grandest of hotels
But, tell me, what are poor parents to do
We would share many wonderful and exciting moments
While visiting famous museums, monuments, parks, and zoos
We'd fulfill countless wishes and make our dreams come true
But, tell me, what are poor parents to do
We would sail the Seven Seas on luxurious yachts
While drifting lazily down the oceans blue
We'd send postcards back home from every port
But, tell me, what are poor parents to do
We would wine and dine in the finest of restaurants
And feast on delicacies from the sea
There would be scrumptious crab, lobster, and a shrimp feast, too
But, tell me, what are poor parents to do
We would shop until we drop in the fanciest of shops
And buy shoes, clothing, and many accessories, too
We would buy gifts and gadgets to give to our friends
But, tell me, what are poor parents to do
We would move into a grand and great big house
And everyone would have his or her very own room
There would be a garden, a pool, a pond, and a tree house, too
But, tell me, what are poor parents to do
The children would attend the finest of schools
And possibly become the next *"Who's Who"*
We may even go back to further our own education
But, tell me, what are poor parents to do
We would give to the poor and those less fortunate
The widows, the orphans, the elderly, the sick, and the homeless, too
We would lift up those who are down in spirit
But, tell me, what are poor parents to do

How do we explain again and again
To sad eyes and downtrodden hearts that are blue
For it breaks our hearts to have to break theirs
So, tell me, please, what are poor parents to do
Now, even though we are not wealthy, affluent, or rich
And maybe these dreams may never come true
But we shall continue to grow humbly in love, hope, and faith
For these are the things that poor parents do
What Poor Parents Do

~ ~ ~

It's Because I Love You

When I try to provide for you a safe and loving home
It's because I love you
When I teach you good manners, morals, and right from wrong
It's because I love you
When I try my best to rear, raise, and train you well
It's because I love you
When I sometimes rant, rage, and raise a whole lot of hell
It's because I love you
When I discipline, punish, reprimand, and chastise you
It's because I love you
When I scold you for some of the things that you say or do
It's because I love you
When I sometimes step back, but not too far, and let you fall
It's because I love you
When I fail to come running every time you call
It's because I love you
When I try to lead you and show you a better way
It's because I love you
When I pray for your soul continuously both night and day
It's because I love you
When I stress the importance of getting an excellent education
It's because I love you
When I share with you The Good News of God's Plan of Salvation
It's Because I Love You
It's Because I Love You

Children Must Be Taught

Children must be taught many, many things . . .

To read and to write
To appreciate the precious gift of life
To listen and to learn
To think on a higher level
To study and discern
To cook and to clean
To be nice and pleasant instead of rude and mean
To respect God, themselves, and others
To honor and obey their fathers and their mothers
To dream big, to brainstorm, and to plan
God's Holy Word and in it to firmly and steadfastly stand
To work productively and industriously
To save wisely and intelligently
To live faithfully and to give graciously
To enjoy the good things in life
To hold on and be strong
In times of turmoil, trouble, and strife
To be kind to the animals, for God left them in our care
To be decent and honest human beings
To be mannerable, polite, forgiving, and fair
To be humble, modest, and meek
To stand proudly on their own two feet
To fear God in a positive and healthy way
And His commandments and laws to always obey
To be good citizens and to get along with others
To live in peace and tranquility amongst their sisters and brothers
To believe in themselves and in the power of the Lord
To have hope and faith and to look forward to the promised reward
To love God first and to love their fellowman as well
To zealously seek God's Kingdom
To help prevent their souls from burning in hell
Yes, children must be taught many, many things
So, let us teach our precious children well
For children must be taught
Children Must Be Taught

Come Inside *Beverly Leonard*

Good Manners for Life

Excuse me, yes ma'am, thank you, please
Yes sir, no sir, cover my mouth when I cough and sneeze
Respect my teachers and be kind to others
My elders, my father, and my mother
Do my best and study hard
Say my prayers to the good Lord
Believe in myself and I will succeed
For there is nothing in this world that I cannot achieve
And these good manners will help me in life
So as I live my life from day to day
These good manners I will always obey
Yes, these good manners I will always obey
Good Manners for Life

~ ~ ~

Under This Roof

Just as the old folks told their children long ago
I'm telling you the very same thing today
Just as long as you live under this roof
You will honor and respect your parents in the same way
Like the old folks use to say back in the day
And if you decide that the rules of our home you won't obey
Then, tough love says it's time for you to get to stepping today
And if you decide to step out into this tough old world
You'll soon realize that what you had here wasn't really so bad
And if it gets too hard out there in life
And you become burdened down by troubles, stress, and strife
Remember, with a renewed attitude, you can always come back home
And if you ever have children of your very own
Honor and respect them and demand the same in your home
And if one day the house rules they wish not to obey
Be sure to tell them what the old folks use to say back in the day
Just as long as you live under this roof, you will obey
Under This Roof

Get an Excellent Education

Young people, get an excellent education
And learn all that you possibly can
For your education will carry you far in life
Yes, it will carry you over sea and land
Even to the ends of the universe
It will help you stretch, excel, soar, and expand
So, young people, get an excellent education
And learn all that you possibly can
Plan and prepare for your future today
For there is really no other way
Set high goals and high expectations
And let nothing and no one mislead you
Or cause you to change directions
Listen, focus, and do your very best
Strive hard and study intensely for every test
Conceive it, believe it, and achieve it
And when you reach your goals in life
Don't forget to reach back
And help someone else along the way
And to them, these very words you, too, must say
Young people, get an excellent education
And prepare for your future today
Get an Excellent Education

~ ~ ~

The Sky Is Not the Limit

Back in the days, the elders would say
"Children, be all that you can be, for the sky is the limit"
Well, now we know that there's a vast universe beyond the sky
So, children, be all that you can be, for beyond the sky you can fly
For, the sky is not the limit
The Sky Is Not the Limit

While You Were Away

While you were away, you missed my birthday
Yes, you missed the day that I was born while you were away
While you were away
You missed my first step, my first word, and my very first tooth
And by the way and just to let you know
My very first word was my attempt at calling out to you
While you were away
While you were away
You missed my very first day of school
And all the parent conferences and programs that I was on
You missed my field trips, my report cards, and even my senior prom
While you were away
While you were away
You missed my graduation when I proudly walked across the stage
While you were away, you missed my coming up of age
While you were away
While you were away
You missed many wonderful moments of my life
My first job and my very first car
My very first love who became my loving wife
My very own home that I could proudly call my own
You missed the births of your grandchildren as well
While you were away, you missed so very much
So much more than mere words can possibly tell
While you were away
While you were away
You missed the many tears that I often shed for you
For you were the only missing piece of the puzzle in my life
And in that vacant spot, no other piece would possibly do
But I thank the Lord that He gave me the perfect peace
The peace of mind that it took to help me make it on through
For He said that He would be a Father to the fatherless ones
And that He'd always be there for His precious daughters and sons
Yes, God has been a good Father to me while you were away
But because I still long for that missing piece in my life
I pray that one day we shall meet
If not on this side of life, then on the other side someday
While You Were Away

You Have a Father

Oh, little child without your dad
I know why you are lonely, depressed, and sad
For you wish that you could have him there with you
To do all the things that dads and their children do
However, for one reason or another, your father went away
Realizing not the depth of the pain and the heartache
That his leaving caused when he left his family that day

Now your heart is broken and you are feeling so much pain
You wonder if you will ever see your father's face ever again
Does he think of you often or not at all
Why doesn't he write, come by, or at least call
For every child needs and deserves two loving parents
For that was the way God planned it to be
A father, a mother, and the children in-between
Yes, this was the holy arrangement for the family

But sometimes things just don't work out as they should
Leaving us hurt, sad, disappointed, lonely, and blue
But, please know, my little one that it is not your fault
And remember that the good Lord is looking down upon you
And God himself said that He would be a Father to the fatherless ones
And please know that no greater Father will you ever find
For God loves and protects His precious daughters and sons

So, little child without your dad
Yes, you have a right to be angry, upset, irate, and even mad
But hold your head up high, my little one, and please stand tall
For your Heavenly Father who loves you so will not let you fall
Be proud of who you are and never ever give up
Though times may get a little bit bumpy and rough
Always say your prayers and do the right thing
And blessings upon you the Lord shall bring
And always remember, my little one, you have a Father
You Have a Father

Come Inside *Beverly Leonard*

Life Is Not Always a Rainbow

Dear Mom and Dad,

The way you treat each other lately really makes me sad
And I long for it to be the way that it was before
When we were a happy and loving family right to the very core
For it breaks my heart to see my family tearing apart
For all children really want is a loving and happy home
To feel safe and secure and to feel that we belong
With two loving parents to lead, nurture, train, and guide
Who will always be here for us standing together side by side
But I'm now old enough to understand and know
That life is not always a rainbow
For, I've lived long enough to understand and see
That with life comes heartache, pain, sadness, and misery
And though I would love to see the two of you together
Loving one another and hanging together tight
Just staying together for the sake of the kids
Doesn't really make it right
For it usually ends up in loud voices, fussing, and cursing
And on a really bad day, maybe in a vicious and violent fight
So, Mom and Dad, please know that I love you both
But I would rather see you living apart
Than tearing at one another's already hurt and fragile heart
Then maybe one day your hearts will be healed
Maybe one day you'll both find true love with another
Just remember always, Mom and Dad, that I love you both
And that you'll always and forever be my father and mother
And though I know that I'm not to blame and that it's not my fault
I'm still sorry that my family just didn't work out
For, life is not always a rainbow

Love and kisses forever

Your child,

Life Is Not Always a Rainbow

Please Don't Count Me Out

Just because my hair is a little bit nappy
And sometimes I come to school a little upset and unhappy
Please don't count me out
Just because my clothes and my shoes
Are not brand-named or brand new
And sometimes they may be a little dirty, too
Please don't count me out
Just because I come to school a little bit late
And cry sometimes because I have a hungry ache
Please don't count me out
Just because I don't catch on as easily as the rest
And do terrible on nearly every test
Please don't count me out
Just because I don't always have my school supplies
And upon others I have to sometimes rely
Please don't count me out
For you know not what my life and my living
Outside of these school walls is all about
For you only see the outside of me
And not the pain and sorrow that I hide deep inside
But if only you knew the heartaches that I go through
Then maybe, just maybe, you'd understand
And instead of putting me down and belittling me
You'd lift me up and give me a helping hand
So, please don't count me out
Please Don't Count Me Out

~ ~ ~

Afterthoughts

Afterthoughts are those thoughts that are thought upon
After our original thoughts have been conceived
Sometimes they make us say, "Hummm"
Because they are so heavy, powerful, and deep
Causing our minds to do quick double takes
Like mental orgasmic earthquakes
Afterthoughts

Through Angel Eyes

Through Angel Eyes
You see the pains, the heartaches, the suffering, and the misery
Of a world that is not as it really should be

Through Angel Eyes
You see a world where bigotry and hatred run long and deep
Even from complete strangers you happen to pass on the streets

Through Angel Eyes
You see families and homes broken, shattered, and torn apart
Enough to break, bend, dent, and splinter even an angel's heart

Through Angel Eyes
You see a world where many people have sold their very souls
For power, prestige, riches, greed, wealth, domination, and control

Through Angel Eyes
You see a world where love doesn't come easy and living is hard
A world that has tuned out and turned away from the good Lord

Through Angel Eyes
You see life as it was originally and ideally meant to be
And it breaks your heart to see all the hurt, the pain, and the misery

But, please know, dear Angel Eyes
That the good Lord's eyes are looking down from Heaven upon you
And that He knows all about the sadness, the hurt, and the pains
That you, dear Angel Eyes, have gone and are still going through

For it is He that has lovingly carried you along the way
And it is He that has promised you a better and brighter day
So, whatever this old world is showing or is failing to show you
By the Lord's holy side, oh, Angel Eyes, please, oh, please, stay

And He who created the Heavens and also the Earth
Shall continue to strengthen, encourage, and help see you through
For, dear Angel Eyes, the Lord has great love for you
Through Angel Eyes

Be Careful Little Children

Be careful little children what you see
For many things that you observe in life
Won't always be as they really should be
So, be careful little children what you see
And from negative sights you must quickly flee

Be careful little children what you hear
For many things that will pass through your ears
Won't always be pleasant, truthful, kind, or nice
So, be careful little children what you hear in this life
And from negative talk you must quickly walk

Be careful little children what you say
For God is listening to you each and every day
So, make sure that your words are honest, kind, and true
For your words will either weigh you down or help uplift you

Be careful little children what you do
For your actions will bring the Lord either sadness or satisfaction
So, do the things that you know in your heart you should
Stay steeped in the Lord's Word and let your living be good

Be careful little children who you call your friends
For many so-called friends won't be there for you in the very end
For, when the goings get tough, they'll be gone
For fair-weathered friends don't last too long

Be careful little children what you learn
For all knowledge is not good knowledge to know
But learn that which will carry you far in life
For, with proper knowledge, wisdom, and understanding
There will be no place that you won't be able to go

And always remember, little children
The good Lord loves and cares for you so
Be Careful Little Children

Come Inside   Beverly Leonard

The Perfect Gift

We give our children so many things
Like toys, computers, cars, and even gold and diamond rings
We give them name-brand sneakers, jerseys, and jackets
Custom-made Christmas stockings and designer Easter baskets
We'd give them the world if only we could
But does all of this giving really do any good
Or does it create spoiled, unruly, and out-of-control kids
Who will more than likely turn out badly and hit the skids
Still, we travel the whole world over
Trying to find that perfect gift to give
Realizing not that the most perfect gift has already been given
In order that we may live
For, God so loved the world that He gave us His only Son
Yes, this was the perfect gift above all others
For there is no greater one
So, parents, please give your children the best present ever
One in which they will never outgrow
For once they come into the knowledge of the Lord
In Him, they will want to live, learn, and forever grow
Parents, please give your children Jesus
The Perfect Gift

~ ~ ~

Motherhood Brings

Motherhood brings . . .

Joy and pain, sunshine and rain
Sorrow and stress, hope and happiness
Worries and fears, heartaches and tears
Pride and jubilation, despair and frustration
The ins and the outs, laughter, screams, and shouts
The ups and the downs, the smiles and the frowns
Good times and bad, the happy and the sad
These are some of the things
That motherhood brings
Motherhood Brings

A Mother's Job Is Never Done

A mother's job is never done
From the early morning sunrise to the setting of the sun
And then throughout the course of the night
To soothe the pains and to chase away the frights
Then she's up in the morning before the roosters crow
For off to work hard-working mothers must go
But not before making sure that everyone is fed
That all is well and that prayers to the good Lord are said
Then she labors at work trying to make the two ends meet
But as hard as she tries, life still tries to knock her off her feet
But she trudges on with the help of the good Lord
For she knows that without Him in her life
Her life and her living would be even more difficult and rock-hard
And though she prays constantly for the welfare of her children
She frets and she worries about them still
For she knows that life is full of trials and tribulations
She knows that life is full of temptations, toils, and dangerous ills
She frets and she worries when they are mere little babes
She frets and she worries until they are lowered into their graves
Then she frets and she worries beyond death and dying
Hoping and praying that her children's souls are saved
Yes, before birth in the delivery room
And beyond death and dying and the memorial tombs
A mother's job is never done
For a mother's job goes on and on
Yes, a mother's job goes on and on
And on and on and on and on
A Mother's Job Is Never Done

~ ~ ~

You Will Always Be My Baby

No matter where you go in life
No matter what you do or how old you get
You will always be my baby
No ifs, ands, buts, or maybes
You Will Always Be My Baby

An Indescribable Feeling

There's an indescribable feeling that parents experience
When their children are in danger, threatened, or being bullied
It's an uncomfortable feeling that abides deep down inside
Where apprehension, worry, fear, dread, and fret reside
A feeling that parents cannot ignore, disregard, or push to the side
And until their children are out of danger and harm's way
Nothing, absolutely nothing is alright and okay
It's an indescribable feeling
Like a knot in the pit of your stomach that just won't go away
Until parents are assured and know that their children are okay
Even if it means sacrificing their lives away
It's an indescribable feeling that just won't go away
Until everything with their children is alright and okay
An Indescribable Feeling

~ ~ ~

The Great Commission

As parents and guardians of our children
We are commissioned by the Lord above
To give them unconditional and dedicated love
To train and to teach, to enlighten and to reach
To feed and to nurture, to love and to hug
To rear and to raise, to lift and to praise
To enhance and to heal, to touch and to feel
To shield, guard, and protect, to build bridges and to connect
To model and to mold, to shape and to hold
To elevate and to inspire, to encourage and to lift higher
To advise and to chastise, to defend and to discipline
To console and to comfort, to soothe and to smooth
To lead and to guide, to be a confidant in which to confide
To understand and to lend a hand, to motivate and to educate
Yes, as parents and guardians of our children
We are commissioned by the Lord above
To do these things for our children
The Great Commission

Oh, Death

Oh, death, where is thy victory
Oh, death, where is thy sting
Oh, death, you should know by now
That Jesus Christ is Lord of Lords and King of Kings
Oh, death, where is thy victory
Oh, death, where is thy sting
Because you've been stung by the Most Holy One
Oh, death, where is thy victory
Oh, death, where is thy sting
Oh, Death

Chapter Six
Death and Dying: Not the Final Chapter

If Tomorrow Never Comes

To my loved ones
If tomorrow never comes
Please know that I love you so
More than mere words can possibly express
More than you'll probably ever know
Please know that I love you so
If tomorrow never comes

To the children of the world
If tomorrow never comes
Please know that you are true gifts from the good Lord above
And that, for you, the Lord has tremendous and great agape love
If tomorrow never comes, my beautiful children
Rise up today and be all that you can be
If tomorrow never comes

To my beautiful Black people all over the world
If tomorrow never comes
Please know that from greatness and grandness we came to be
And that we possess a proud and glorious heritage and history
And it's time for our people to rise out of our oppression and misery
Today, we must join together as One People in solidarity and unity
If tomorrow never comes

To those who hate their fellow man
Simply because of the color of their skin
Please know that if you continue to hate instead of love
Then into the eternal flames your soul shall surely descend
If tomorrow never comes, oh, bigots of the world
Then today you'd better change your bitter and hateful ways
If tomorrow never comes

To all the people of the world
If tomorrow never comes
Let us love one another as God said we should
Let us do unto one another that which is righteous, true, and good
Let us put the Lord first in all that we do
And everything else shall be added unto me and to you

If Tomorrow Never Comes

Come Inside *Beverly Leonard*

You May Not Have Tomorrow

If you need to tell someone that you love them
Tell them you love them today
For you may not have tomorrow
The opportunity these words to say
So, tell them that you love them today

If you need to forgive someone for trespassing against you
Forgive them for trespassing against you today
For you may not have tomorrow to heal old wounds
Besides, if we are to be forgiven for the wrongs that we've done
Then we, too, must forgive others in the same forgiving way
So, forgive those who have trespassed against you today

If you need to ask someone's forgiveness for the wrongs you've done
Ask them to forgive you today
For you may not have tomorrow in which to ask them
So, ask them while these words you can still say
Ask for forgiveness today

If you need to be more compassionate, caring, and kind
As well as benevolent toward your fellow man
Do these things today while you still yet can
For you may not have tomorrow to do these things
So, show these godly qualities today toward your fellow man

If you need to teach and reach the minds and hearts of someone
In order to show them a better way
Teach and reach their minds and hearts today
For you may not have tomorrow to teach and reach them
So, teach and reach them today

If you have not come to know the good Lord
Come to know the good Lord today
For you may not have tomorrow to come to know Him
And you'll miss your opportunity to live forever within His holy realm
So, if you have not come to know the good Lord
Take time out today to come to know Him
For, you may not have tomorrow
You May Not Have Tomorrow

Life Is But a Fleeting Moment

Life is but a fleeting moment
One day we're here and the next day we're gone
For, like the sweet morning dew that soon fades away
Life on the Earth doesn't last too long
One day we're here and the next day we're gone
Life is but a fleeting moment
So, while we can, let us love our fellow man as we know we should
Let us do unto others that which is righteous, true, and good
Let us love God first with our whole mind, soul, and heart
And from the safety of His holy realm let us never depart
Life is but a fleeting moment
So, while we still can, let us forgive our fellow man
For, it is written, that in order to be forgiven, we must first forgive
If in Paradise with the Lord, we hope to eternally live
So, while we still can, let us forgive our fellow man
Life is but a fleeting moment
So, let us cherish the time that we have with our loved ones
Let us not take this time simply for granted
For, before we know it, the death angels shall surely come
And let us thank the Lord for the time that He gives us
To spend with our friends and our beloved ones
Life is but a fleeting moment
So, while we are here, let us learn our lessons well
For, according to our deeds done upon the Earth
We shall live eternally in Paradise or spend eternity in Hell
So, let us learn our lessons and learn them well
Life is but a fleeting moment
Therefore, let us not waste our precious time
On things that are small, trivial, insignificant, and trite
But let us keep our minds stayed and focused on the things
That will lead us and bring us closer and closer to The Light
Closer to the One who shall soon restore life as it was meant to be
To be lived in peace, love, and laughter-ever-after eternally
But until that time comes, life is but a fleeting moment
Life Is But a Fleeting Moment

Come Inside   *Beverly Leonard*

The Rushing Of Time

The seconds rush into the minutes
The minutes rush into the hours
The hours rush into the days
The days rush into the weeks
The weeks rush into the months
The months rush into the years
There's definitely a rushing of time

It's Monday morning and you're back at work
The weekend came and away it went
You just paid the bills trying to get caught up
But before you know it, it's time once again to pay the rent
You rush here and there trying to beat or meet the deadlines
Schedules, meetings, and appointments
Yes, there's definitely a rushing of time

A baby is born and before you know it
She has a family of her very own
But it seems like only yesterday
That with her dolls and her toys she did play
And now the little baby is all grown
You look into the mirror and into the eyes of old age
When only yesteryear, you were young and carefree
And now you're approaching your final stage

Yes, it seems as though the Earth
Is spinning faster and faster around the sun
For, the more we try, the harder it seems to get things done
Or maybe we simply do too much
Cramming everything into the hours
For, we've forgotten how to live simple and happy lives
We've forgotten how to stop and smell the flowers

But no longer can we afford to waste our precious time
On things that are trivial, small, minute, and trite
For time has a way of rushing right by us
Yes, time, like an eagle, takes on flight
The Rushing Of Time

Temporary Living

In these days and times nothing seems to last forever
They're here one day and the next day they're gone
For temporary things change like the weather
Temporary homes and temporary families
Broken, abandoned, and depleted
Temporary proposals and temporary plans
Temporary projects never to be completed
Temporary friendships, feelings, and affections
Temporary arrangements and temporary connections
Temporary jobs and temporary careers
Temporary mind-sets and temporary fears
Temporary fortunes, fame, and wealth
Temporary happiness and temporary health
Temporary church homes and temporary schools
Temporary laws and temporary rules
Temporary leaders promising to do what is right
But changing their agendas once out of sight
Temporary knowledge that changes over time
Temporary beliefs creating mixed-up minds
Temporary peace and temporary solutions
Destroying the world with all sorts of pollutions
Some people even claim temporary deaths
And brief glimpses of the other side
They speak of a place beyond compare
A place where temporary doesn't reside
A place of everlasting love and security
Where peaceful and gentle waters flow
A place where joy fills the hearts
A place where I would love to one day go
So, I'll accept this temporary living with Heaven on my mind
Loving God first and my also my sisters and my brothers
So that one day Heaven I shall find
And thank God that this old world is only temporary
For this old world is full of heartache, trouble, and strife
But through God's only begotten Son, Jesus Christ
There is hope for everlasting life
For this old life is only temporary
Temporary Living

One of These Old Days

One of these old days
You're going to look for me and I'll be gone
My earthly body I'll leave behind
But my spirit shall return to my heavenly home
Yes, one of these old days
You're going to look for me and I'll be gone
One of these old days
The Lord is going to call my name
And I hope to be ready to meet my Maker
And my heavenly robe I hope to be able to claim
Yes, one of these old days
The Lord is going to call my name
One of these old days
The angels of the Lord will come to meet me
To carry me home where my spirit belongs
Where peace, joy, and love reside eternally
Yes, one of these old days
The angels of the Lord will come to meet me
One of these old days
I'll be reunited with my loved ones who've gone on before me
We'll sing, dance, and shout glory hallelujah
And give God all the praise, the honor, and the glory
Yes, one of these old days
I'll be reunited with my loved ones who've gone on before me
Yes, one of these old days
You're going to look for me and I'll be gone
My earthly body I'll leave behind
But my spirit shall return to my heavenly home
Yes, one of these old days
You're going to look for me and I'll be gone
But until that day comes
In the Lord's holy and righteous realm, I shall strive to stay
So that when He calls my name
I won't end up going the opposite way
One of These Old Days

If You Were To Die This Very Moment

If you were to die this very moment
Would your house be found in order
Or would it be found in a cluttered and tangled-up mess
Will your spirit be able to find peace
Or will it be unable to find eternal rest
If you were to die this very moment
Would you have forgiven those who have done you wrong
Or will death find you still angry, bitter, and full of malice
And onto grudges, hatred, and hostilities will you still be holding on
If you were to die this very moment
Would you have loved enough to cover a multitude of sins
Or will your sins outweigh the love you have shown
Toward your sisters and your brethren
If you were to die this very moment
Would you have helped to spread God's Holy Word
Would you have brought someone closer to the Lord above
By sharing the Good News of His Kingdom and of His awesome love
If you were to die this very moment
Would you be found righteous with the Lord
Would your name be found in The Book of Life
Would you be ready to receive your heavenly reward
If you were to die this very moment
Would you be able to stand in the very end
Would you live forever and always in Paradise
Or into the flames of hell would your soul descend
If you were to die this very moment
Would your house be found in order
Or would it be found in a cluttered and tangled-up mess
Will your spirit be able to find peace
Or will it be unable to find eternal rest
If an orderly house is not what the Lord will find
Then you'd better clean your house up now
While there is still yet time
If You Were To Die This Very Moment

Come Inside   *Beverly Leonard*

When We're Busy Making Plans

Someone once said:

"Life is what happens when we're busy making plans"
~
It was a Friday afternoon and the party would be the very next day
And busy as bees were we just happily planning away
There would be food, music, plenty of fun, and many party favors
There would be chips and dips, cold drinks, and many daiquiri flavors
Yes, busy as bees were we as we prepared for the party
But then the phone call came and our plans did change
Because, for our dear and beloved mother, the Angels of Death came
And instead of planning a party
We had to plan for a funeral instead
Yes, life is what happens when we're busy making plans
Just like that someone once said
When We're Busy Making Plans

~ ~ ~

The Blue Period

Pablo Picasso went through a period in his life
When he depicted many scenes of sadness, suffering, sorrow, and strife
And during this particular period of his life
Everything that he drew was dipped and shaded in the color blue
And now I, "The Poet with a Message"
Present my Blue Period of Poetry to you
The Blue Period

The Phone Call

It was a Friday afternoon and all was well
Until I received a frantic phone call
That caused my mind to spin, swirl, and twirl
For the weakened heart of my dear mom had come to a sudden stop
Which caused the blood that flows to her brain to be blocked
But the paramedics came and her heartbeat they did reclaim
But the life of my beloved mother would never be the same
For, never again would she open her eyes and smile
Never again would she call out my name
Now my heart is full of sorrow, sadness, and pain
The Phone Call

~ ~ ~

The Machines

Though it seems as if she is breathing on her on
It is really the machines that is lengthening her life along
But how long could, would, and should this go on
For I knew in my heart that my mother wouldn't be returning home
At least not to her earthly home
For her spirit was tired and now ready to move on
Therefore, the unavoidable and inescapable question arose
To unplug or not
Such a decision to make is such a hard and heavy lot
The Machines

The Death Angels Come

The Angels of Death have come and are present in the room
For I can feel their powerful and peaceful presence
Though my heart is filled with great sadness and gloom
And all around stands family, kin, and family friends
All hoping and praying that our beloved one will awaken once again
But all knowing in our hearts that she is near her earthly end
And that a new journey for our beloved one will soon begin
For her spirit is tired, weary, and weak, and her body cannot go on
So, the Angels of Death have been commissioned by the good Lord
To come and carry my beloved mother safely home
Waiting ever so patiently for us to say our final good-byes
Before our precious one succumbs to death and dies
The Death Angels Come

~ ~ ~

Death Cometh

No longer can we prolong the inevitable
For, when death calls, unto death we all must fall
So, the decision is made and we think it is best
To end her suffering and allow her spirit to find rest
So, the plugs are pulled and our hearts are heavy and full
Full of pain, sadness, sorrow, and misery
For, no longer upon the Earth, our loved one we shall see
Yes, death cometh to receive my beloved one
To receive her spirit and carry it safely home
Death Cometh

~ ~ ~

A River of Tears

God blesses Mankind with the ability to produce tears
To help sooth our hurts and pains and to help ease our fears
Thank you, oh, Lord, for your mercy and for your grace
For I cry a long river of tears
A River of Tears

Death Came

Soon death came and the life of my beloved one it did claim
And I cried and I cried and I cried and I cried
When my dear and beloved mother passed away and died
And after many, many tears, I came to realize
That the tears that I shed were not really for the dead
But the tears that I shed were for me instead
For my beloved one have gone on to a far better place
But I will miss her laughter, her smile, and her beautiful face
Yes, the tears that I shed are not for the dead
But they are for me instead
Death Came

~ ~ ~

At The Graveside

I stood at the graveside of my dear and beloved mother
And cried a river of tears that flowed from a sad and broken heart
For life had not been the same since my beloved one did depart
For death is a hard pill to swallow, but swallow it, we all must
For mere mortals all are we and we all must return to dust
For it is written that death has been appointed to everyone
Which means that unto everyone, death shall surely come
And while standing at the graveside of my beloved one
I thought of Jesus' mother Mary and the other women
Who went to the graveside of God's only begotten Son
And what they beheld that day caused them great fear
For the angel of the Lord was there
And the angel asked them, "Why are you here"
I then realized that my beloved one was not there
And that she had moved on to her heavenly home
And that from the graveside, it was time for me to move on
At The Graveside

I Miss You Mama

I miss you Mama
More than mere words can possibly say
I miss you Mama with each and every passing day
For something that reminds me of you always come my way
Be it a song, a scent, a special occasion, or a particular event
Or maybe a recollection of something funny that you did or did say
Something that reminds me of you always comes my way
Sometimes I smile and sometimes I laugh
Sometimes I break down and cry
Sometimes I even ask the Lord, "Lord, oh, Lord, why"
Knowing in my heart that God knows what's best
He knew that it was time for you to come home and find rest
Still, I miss you Mama
I Miss You Mama

~ ~ ~

I Can't Call My Mama

I can't call my Mama like I use to do
To ask her how was her day
Or just to say, "Mama, I love you"
No, I can't call my Mama like I use to do
I Can't Call My Mama

~ ~ ~

When Will the Pain Pass

When will the hurt stop
When will the pain pass
Will my heart heal with time
Or will the hurt and the heartaches forever last
Tell me, when will the pain past
When Will the Pain Pass

The Holiday Blues

The holidays are quickly approaching and drawing near
And by my side, dear Mother, you won't be here
Tell me, Mother, what am I going to do to get through without you
I know I'll have the holiday blues
The Holiday Blues

~ ~ ~

From Dust

From dust we are and to dust we shall return
But that which is spiritual shall move on
Some to a place of total darkness and doom
Some to a heavenly and holy home
Yes, the physical returns back to dust from whence it came
But that which is spiritual moves on
From Dust

~ ~ ~

Sooner or Later

Sooner or later we all must die
And sin is the root and the reason why
That sooner or later we all must die
But death won't have the last and final say
That will be left up to the Lord on Judgment Day
Sooner or Later

~ ~ ~

From Blue to Rose

Pablo Picasso's Blue Period lasted four long years
When he depicted scenes of sadness, sorrow, grief, and tears
But then one day true love came his way
And soon the color blue became rose that helped brighten his day
But every now and then when depression and despair would set in
Picasso would revisit the Blue Period once again
And now, like Picasso, I will bring my Blue Period to an end
But I suspect that, like Picasso, I, too, shall revisit this period again
From Blue to Rose

On Borrowed Time

We're all living on borrowed time
For time belongs to the good Lord above
Who gives it out as He sees fit
For He is the Creator and the Grantor of it
Yes, we're all living on borrowed time
It doesn't belong to you nor is it mine
For, we're all living on borrowed time
On Borrowed Time

~ ~ ~

Dying To Live

I'm dying and so are you
For such are the wages and the penalties of sin
For ever since that day when true joy and peace went away
Dying is the way that it's always been
But there is a glorious and resurrected hope found only in the Lord
And everlasting-life-after-death is the everlasting reward
So, let us all come to know the love of the good Lord
And great and glorious shall be our eternal reward
Dying To Live

~ ~ ~

Before The Curtains Close

Before Old Man Winter comes
And the cold arctic winds begin to blow
The beauty of the autumn leaves captivates our visual senses
And gives us a spectacular and breath-taking show
The awesome arrays of colors are so beautiful to behold
They bring joy to our hearts and delight to our souls
Like a grand finale before the curtains close
Before The Curtains Close

Before I Die And Leave This Old World

Before I die and leave this old world
And move on to yet another
I must try to make a positive difference in this world
Yes, I must do what I can to help uplift my sisters and my brothers
Before I die and leave this old world and move on to yet another
Before I die and leave this old world
I must rear, raise, teach, and train my children well
I must help them to be the very best they can be
Besides, this will help prevent their souls from burning in hell
Yes, before I die and leave this old world
I must rear, raise, teach, and train my children well
Before I die and leave this old world
I want to see my Black people set free
Set free from oppression, suffering, injustice, and inequality
Set free from the binding and blinding mindset caused by slavery
Yes, before I die and leave this old world
I want to see my beautiful Black people set free
Before I die and leave this old world
I want to see bigotry, hatred, and racism come to an end
I want to see the fulfillment of Dr. King's Dream
That one day Mankind will walk together hand in hand
Yes, before I die and leave this old world
I want to see bigotry, hatred, and racism come to an end
Before I die and leave this old world
I want to help spread love, hope, and the joy found only in the Lord
For His yolk is light, refreshing, gentle, and kind
While this old world's yolk is cruel, harsh, heavy, and hard
Yes, before I die and leave this old world
I want to help spread love, hope, and the joy found only in the Lord
Before I die and leave this old world
I want to make sure that I love a lot
For love covers a multitude of sins
And sins are what we've all got
Yes, before I die and leave this old world
I want to make sure that I love a lot
Before I Die And Leave This Old World

The Setting of the Sun

There's something special about the setting of the sun
And its brilliance and beauty that stretches across the horizon
Maybe it's the magnificent colors all aglow and set ablaze
Maybe it's the dynamic dimensions of the sculptured rays
Maybe it reminds us of our Creator who created the sunset just so
So that of His majesty and of His glory we all would come to know
Maybe it reminds us of death and our inevitable end
Maybe it reminds us of life after death
When our spiritual journey shall begin
Yes, there's something special
About the setting
Of the
Sun
The Setting of the Sun

~ ~ ~

I'm Going Home

The Angels of Death have come to receive my spirit
For, my body is weary and weak and cannot continue on
So the Death Angels have been commissioned by the good Lord
To come down to the Earth and carry my spirit safely home
Now, while lying here in this sickbed unmoving and eyes closed
I sense their powerful and spiritual presence as never before
As they quietly and patiently linger outside my door
Causing me to come to terms with the terms of death and dying
Causing me to realize that death is a natural part of the whole
And that in order to move on to my next spiritual journey
This earthly journey must now end and come to a final close
And now I look forward to my spiritual journey home
To be with the Lord who still sits on his heavenly throne
So, death, come on in, and Angels let us be on our way
For, no longer upon the Earth do I wish to tarry or stay
I'm Going Home

Going Through

If I happen to out-live my loved ones
That would mean that I would have to go through
The heartaches and the pains of the deaths of those I love
Just the thought itself is quite overwhelming and hard
So hard, in fact, it makes me want to shout, "Oh, my Lord"
And, on the other hand, if my loved ones live longer than me
Then the same heartaches and pains, they, too, shall surely see
It seems that heartaches and pains are just plain raw realities
We all shall lose those we love; it's just a fact of life
For, when sin entered in, life became filled with heartache and strife
Now, I've looked upon the lives of many who've lost loved ones before
And I've often wondered just how they have made it through
And I've noticed that each of them possess strong faith in the Lord
And they proclaim that without the Lord to help pull them through
They just wouldn't know what to do, and I know this to be true
Because it is my faith in the Lord that helps pull me through
Yes, whether I shall out-live my loved ones
Or whether I shall pass on before them
Heartache and pain shall surely be here
But it's so good to know that God still loves us so
And that in times of heartache and pain
He will strengthen us and fill our hearts with good cheer
Going Through

~ ~ ~

In My Sleep

When I die, oh, Lord, please let me die in my sleep
Please let me pass on to the other side
When my heart, mind, and soul are calm and at peace
Yes, when I die, oh, Lord, please let me die peacefully in my sleep
In My Sleep

Come Inside   *Beverly Leonard*

When I'm Gone

When I'm gone, please let me go
Please release me to go on to a place I've never been before
When I'm gone, moan for me if you must
Release the tears and let them flow
For, through our tears, we live, we learn, and we grow
When I'm gone, please carry on and give life your very best
Don't give up, give in, or give out
But press on despite life's many trials, tribulations, and tests
When I'm gone, think of me every now and then
And may the memories that I leave behind
Great comfort and solace in them I hope you shall find
When I'm gone, please remember to pray for one another
And to always show true love and compassion
To all of your sisters and brothers
When I'm gone, cling to the hope that we shall see one another again
For the Lord has promised a glorious resurrection
To those who shall remain faithful until the very end
So, when I'm gone, please let me go
Please release me to go on to a place I've never been before
And let us thank the good Lord for the time that we had together
When I'm Gone

~ ~ ~

The Last Trip

We shall travel many roads in life
Some will lead to joy and happiness
While others will lead to sadness, heartache, and strife
But there is one road that we all must journey
And that's the road that leads to the cemetery
So, as we travel the highways and the byways of life
Let us be mindful to guard our hearts in order to save it
So that on that day when our spirit slips away
It shall return to the One who gave it
The Last Trip

Until We See One Another Again

To My Loved Ones

If I should die before you
Please be strong and continue to hold on
And remember to call upon the good Lord
To help lift you up and help make you strong
And in the strength that the Lord shall provide unto you
Please thank Him for the time that we had together
And in the sweet memories that I leave behind
Great comfort and solace in them, I pray that you shall find
Until we meet again someday
This I pray
And, on the other hand, if you should die before I do
I'll pray and ask the Lord to please strengthen me
And help lift me up and help carry me through
For my heart shall be sad, shattered, and broken
Yes, my heart shall be heavily laden from missing you
And in the strength that the Lord shall provide unto me
I'll thank Him for the time that we had together
And in the sweet memories that you leave behind
Great comfort and solace in them, I shall find
Until we see one another again some day
This I pray
Until We See One Another Again

~ ~ ~

Over, Said, and Done

When my life down here is over, said, and done
My spirit shall return to my heavenly home
To be with my Heavenly Father and his beloved Son
When my life down here is over, said, and done
Over, Said, and Done

The Obituary

They peer back at me each and every day
Wearing happy, content, and smiling faces
As if happy to leave this old world behind
And move on to higher spiritual places
Yes, they peer back at me with happy, contented, and smiling faces
And I know that one day the Death Angels will come for me
Then, it will be my smiling face in the obituary you will see
Peering back at you and happy to have made it safely through
The Obituary

~ ~ ~

The Wake

They came in one-by-one and two-by-two
To pay their last respects, and the body of the deceased to view
To sit with the family who were sad and broken-hearted
To comfort and console the loved ones of the dearly departed
And the Inspired Word of the Lord was spoken and shared
So were words about the departed one from those who cared
But those who came couldn't sit too long in the room
For another wake would be happening real soon
In fact, there was a constant flow in and out of the visiting room
For, death does not sleep, oh, no, it is always awake
As the souls of Mankind it strikes down and overtakes
The Wake

~ ~ ~

The Black Dress

The black dress hangs in the back of the closet
Waiting patiently until the next funeral it shall attend
Yes, the black dress waits patiently in the back of the closet
Knowing that sooner or later death will strike once again
The Black Dress

And May It Be Said

When I die and leave this old world and move on to yet another
I hope that it may be said about the life that I led
That I was a loving mate, daughter, sister, aunt, and mother
And may it be said about the life that I led
That I was a true and trusted friend
One who was there in both good times and bad
One who extended a listening ear and also a helping hand
And may it be said about the life that I led
That I inspired and encouraged others along life's way
To be the very best that they could possibly be
And that, away from trouble and adversity, they should stay
And may it be said about the life that I led
That I was a warrior for righteousness sake
That I tried to promote peace, love, and understanding
And that I was genuine and true and not false or fake
And may it be said about the life that I led
That I was caring, humble, modest, and meek
That I never maliciously or intentionally caused harm to anyone
And that brotherhood and sisterhood is what I did seek
And may it be said about the life that I led
That I was respectful, courteous, honest, and kind
And that I tried to instill these values into others as well
That I tried to motivate, enlighten, and enhance the human mind
And may it be said about the life that I led
That I clung to hope and that my faith in the Lord was strong
And though far from perfect, I tried to do my very best
To do what was right and stay away from wrong
And may it be said about the life that I led
That I helped to bring someone closer to the good Lord
For, if this be so, then in the Lord they will grow
And great and wonderful will be my heavenly reward
Yes, when I die and leave this old world
And move on to yet another
I hope that these things can be said
About the life that I once led
And May It Be Said

Scared To Die

He said that he was scared to die
And I wondered why he was scared to die
Maybe he was scared to die because he lived his life steeped in sin
Maybe he was scared to die because he believed
That into the hellfire his soul would descend in the very end
Maybe he was scared to die because faith and hope he lacked
Maybe he was scared to die because he thought death was final
And that there will be is nothing after that
Maybe he was scared to die because unto God and his fellow man
No true love, caring, and compassion were shown
Maybe he was scared to die because he knew that one day
He would have to stand in judgment before God's holy throne
Yes, he said that he was scared to die
And it made me wonder why he was scared to die
Oh, ye who is scared to die
Please listen to these words of wisdom that cometh from on high
The Lord of Hosts says, "Beloved, you don't have to be scared to die"
If you're living your life steeped in sin
Repent **NOW** while there is still yet time and turn your life around
No longer allow sin and satan to weigh your spirit down
Seek ye first God's Kingdom now while it still can be found
If faith and hope are what you lack
Then it's time to get these essential elements back on track
Of God's holy and righteous Word, you must quickly come to know
And, like tiny mustard seeds, your faith and hope will grow
It you think that death is the final journey of the soul
Please know that death is simply a part of the whole
For the spirit that God blew into Mankind that day
It doesn't die, oh, no, but it's the physical part that passes away
But the soul of Mankind lives on and on and on and on
And shall eventually reside forever in hell or in a heavenly home
If you have not loved like you know you should
Start loving right now and unto others be kind, loving, and good
For love shall cover a multitude of our sins
So, don't be caught short of love in the very end
That way, when the Lord calls you before his holy thrown
Your sins will be covered by the love that you have shown

Therefore, turn from your sinful ways
Seek and find the Lord while He still can be found today
Read, believe, and in His holy and righteous Word heed
Know that death is simply a part of the whole
Love God with your whole mind, heart, and soul
And also love your fellow man
So that on that great day when the Lord calls your name
You, my beloved one, shall be able to stand
You Don't Have To Be Scared To Die

~ ~ ~

If a Man Dies

If a man dies, shall he live again?   *Job 14:14*

If a man dies, shall he live again
Well, that all depends upon the man
And how much he loved and how he lived his life upon the Earth
If he lived his life outside of the Lord's holy realm
Then death, doom, and destruction shall surely befall him
If he loved God first and also his fellow man
Then, yes, he shall surely live again
Therefore, if a man dies and lives again
Depends on how he lived and loved God and his fellow man
And upon the mighty, mighty mercy and grace of God above
Who, for Mankind, still has great and tremendous agape love
If a Man Dies

~ ~ ~

In Every City and Town

Cemeteries can be found in every city and in every town
Yes, in every city and in every town cemeteries can be found
Which means that no matter where we go, here or there
Death and dying abound and can be found everywhere
In Every City and Town

Come Inside *Beverly Leonard*

The Pope Has Died
In memory of Pope John Paul II

The Pope has died
The Pope has died
And all around the world millions of people cried
Because their beloved Pope John Paul has died
For the world has lost a holy and an up-right man of God
Who, for 27 years, faithfully led God's earthly flock
A humble man whose love for his fellow man was solid as a rock
Deeply loved by both the poor and also the rich
"He was a wise and fearless leader," said the U.S. President
He walked with remarkable courage, charisma, and confidence
A leader who taught and led by fine examples was he
Exemplifying love, love of life, forgiveness, compassion, and unity
Who spread love and hope both far and near
Bringing blessings of peace and tidings of joy and good cheer
Even after he was wounded by a sniper's bullet
Whom this gracious man did forgive
He continued to travel in his Pope Mobile until he became too ill
And his Heavenly Father who looked down from Heaven above
Upon His faithful and beloved servant, Pope John
Said, "Come home, my son, for your work upon the Earth is done
For your spirit has grown tired, weary, weak, and worn
You have ran a good race, now it's time to come home"
Yes, today, many people around the world cried
Because their beloved Pope John Paul has died
The flags now fly at half-staff, and the candles, they are lit
Vigils are held in masses, and many prayers to the Lord are sent
The bells ring out from all around
And not many a dry eye among the flock can be found
For their beloved Pope has died today
Yes, from the Earth, this gentle spirit has gone away
Now, who will lead God's earthly flock
Who will be their leader, their guide, and their rock
For, the Pope has died
The Pope has died
And all round the world millions of people cried
The Pope has died
The Pope Has Died

Calling All Black People

SOS...SOS...SOS...SOS...SOS...SOS...SOS...SOS
This is an emergency
This is an emergency
Calling all of God's beautiful Black people under the sun
For it is time for the Sleeping Giants to awaken and arise
It is time to regain our dignity, our self-esteem, our honor, and our pride
It is time to come together in unity and stand together as one
For this is the only way that the salvation of our people can be done
So, this call goes out to all of God's beautiful Black people
To all of God's beautiful Black people under the sun
Who have been scattered here and there over land and sea
Your Heavenly Father says, "It's time to come together in unity
It's time to come back and return to Me"
Calling all Black people
Calling all Black people
SOS...SOS...SOS...SOS...SOS...SOS...SOS...SOS
This is an emergency
This is an emergency
Calling All Black People

Chapter Seven
From the Depths of my Blackness

Many Races, Yet, One Mankind

Black   **White**
And every shade in-between
Many races you will certainly find
Each diverse, unique, and different
Yet, originating from one Mankind
Created by the same Grand Master Creator
Who created both the Heavens and also the Earth
Who blew into Mankind the Spirit of Life
On the day of Mankind's blessed and glorious birth
Black   **White**
And every shade in-between
Many Races, Yet, One Mankind

~ ~ ~

February is . . .

February is a special time
A time to reflect on life and love
The love of family and the love of friends
The love of the Lord that surpasses and transcends
A time to reflect on the past that has brought us here today
A time to sing, shout, rejoice, release, and pray
A time to come together as one and try to find a better way
Yes, February is a special time
February should be every day
February is . . .

~ ~ ~

Great Love

Now, please don't get me wrong, for I have love for all people
For, through God's blood, we are all made one - One People
But I must confess that I have *Great Love* for my Black people
Yes, for my beautiful Black people, I have *Great Love*
Great Love

The Treasure Chest

There once was a beautiful treasure chest
Filled with many gems, jewels, and precious stones
But then one day it was pilfered and plundered
Until all of its beauty and riches were depleted and gone

It was taken to a far off and distant land
Where it was mistreated far worse than an old tin can
Beaten and bashed and treated like trash
The once beautiful treasure chest could now barely stand

And no longer did it sparkle, shine, glimmer, or glow
And, over time, the beauty and richness of its past it did not know
And this void was filled with lies, deceit, humiliation, and shame
Shame of what it was and shame of whence it came

But there was something about this treasure chest
Something that stirred from deep, deep within
Something that transcended the misery and despair that it was in
It was the Spirit of the treasure chest that kept it alive
Yes, it was the Spirit of the treasure chest that helped it to survive

For beneath the dust, the dirt, and the built-up grime
Beneath all of the bitter and twisted lies that it had been told
Was a magnificent masterpiece of sheer and splendid beauty
Simply exquisite to behold

For how long can lies live before truths are revealed
And soon the treasure chest regained its self-esteem and pride
But it longed for its precious treasures that it once held inside
And this emptiness and longing it could no longer hide

Oh, jewels, gems, and precious stones
You who have been scattered over land and sea
The treasure chest awaits your glorious return
It says, "Come home, my precious ones
Come home and return to Me"
The Treasure Chest

Come Inside   *Beverly Leonard*

Africa and Her Children

Africa was a strong Black woman - Queen of all the land
Her storehouses overflowed with riches and wealth
In the great land we now call Sudan
She was blessed with many children
True gifts from the good Lord above
And she watched them grow in strength and might
While showering them with her undying love

But then one day the strangers came
Bearing whips, guns, shackles, and chains
And with hatred and bitterness in their eyes
Africa's children they soon laid claim
Never was there such sadness, weeping, and a' wailing
Heard in all the land
For the enslavement of Africa's children
Was more than Mother Africa could stand

Now, the other Mother Countries did nothing to stop her pain
Only stood by and watched the mayhem and the madness
For Africa's loss were their selfish and greedy gain
They took her loved ones far away to a land far beyond the sea
Then filled them with terrors and horrors beyond compare
Yes, filled them with oppression, injustice, cruelty, and misery

Neither Africa nor her children have been the same since that day
When they pilfered all her storehouses and carried her children away
And their cries for one another can still be heard all around
For justice and the true human spirit have yet to be found

But their strong inner spirit
Granted from the Greatest Spirit on High
Refused to give up, give in, or give out
Yes, their strong inner spirit refused to die
And it is this same inner spirit that will lift them once again
And reunite Mother Africa and her children
To their once proud and native homeland
Africa and Her Children

Come Inside   *Beverly Leonard*

A Message from Mother Africa

I am Great Mother Africa
The Queen Mother of all civilizations
For upon my great and grand continent
You could find the original Black nations

My storehouses overflowed with riches and wealth
As we enjoyed good living, good fortune, and also good health
My children were strong, intelligent, proud, and wise
And it was here in Great Mother Africa that great pyramids were built
And the Arts and the Sciences came alive

Many nations would come from both far and near
To learn from my gifted Black daughters and sons
For my children were the pioneers of medicine and engineering
Yes, they came to Mother Africa to see just how it should be done

But then one day the strangers came
And took my precious children away in chains
They took them to a land far beyond the Mid-Atlantic Sea
And threw them into the bitter bowels of bondage and slavery

And life has never been quite the same ever since that day
When they stole upon my shores and took my children away
***Sh*...** Oh, listen
I can still hear the cries of my children
For they are still oppressed, held down, and in pain
For even though the physical chains were removed
The mental effects of slavery still to this day remain

Oh, listen, my beautiful Black children
You who have been tossed and scattered over land and sea
Your Mother says, "It's time to awaken and arise
And regain your once-strong self-esteem, pride, and dignity
And always remember that you came from greatness and glory
After all, my beautiful Black children, you came from me"
A Message from Mother Africa

My Family Tree

My family tree has many splintered, spl-it, broken, torn and unknown branches, which have caused for me, in my search to know my history, great frustration, aggravation, exasperation, anguish, and misery, stemming from my lack of knowledge concerning my family tree. But the good Lord looked down from Heaven above and felt my sorrow, my heartache, and my misery. And this is what the Master one day said to me, concerning the missing branches on my family tree. He said, "My precious child, you fail to grasp and realize just whose orchard your family tree is planted in. And when you come to this realization and truth, this wisdom will create great joy and pride within. In fact, it will cause your heart to overflow with gladness, and it will wipe away all of your sorrows and sadness, to know that your family tree directly connects back to me. So, despite the many details and specifics that you may lack, please know this most important and essential fact - your family tree belongs to Me. And this truth shall set you free. Now with this knowledge deeply embedded in your heart, soul, and mind, spread your roots far and wide, my child, and you'll be just fine, right where you are on your family tree." This is what the Lord said to me concerning my family tree
My Family Tree

Because I'm Here Today

Because I'm here today
I know that my ancestors were caught and captured
Along the western shores of the great continent called Africa
Shackled and chained, beaten, battered, and pained
Yes, because I am here today
I know that from Mother Africa my ancestors came

Because I'm here today
I know that my ancestors were a strong and courageous people
For they survived the deadly voyage across the Mid-Atlantic Sea
In wooden tombs of death, doom, and destruction
Filled with sadness, sorrow, horror, fright, and misery
Yes, because I'm here today
I know that my ancestors were a strong and courageous people

Because I'm here today
I know that my people are survivors
For we have survived through four hundred *plus* years
Of constant oppression, exploitation, dehumanization
Death, blood, sweat, and tears
Yes, because I'm here today
I know that my people are survivors

Because I'm here today
I know that God has a special purpose planned for my life
So, I must continue to climb this up-hill journey
Despite my trials, my tribulations, my troubles, and my strife
Yes, because I'm here today
I know that God has a special purpose planned for my life

Because I'm here today
I know that God has great love for me
And that without His goodness, His mercy, and His saving grace
My life just would not be
But because I am here today
I know for a fact that the Lord has great love for me
These things I know because I'm here today
Because I'm Here Today

When We Had Less

When we had less we really had more
More love for God, for ourselves, and for others
When we had less we really had more
More respect for our neighbors, our fathers, and our mothers
When we had less we really had more
We thirsted for knowledge, wisdom, and true understanding
We fought for justice and equality in a divided land
And because we were united as one, we were able to stand
When we had less we really had more
We had strong Black families where God was the head
And though the storms raged on, our families stayed strong
For if God is the head, then who can be misled
When we had less we really had more
We had a united community that came together as one
A safe cocoon in which to live, love, and grow
And there were no problems the village could not overcome
When we had less we really had more
We endured and persevered through the trials of this old life
We didn't give up, give in, or give out
We pressed on despite our troubles, tribulations, and strife
When we had less we really had more
We had more self-esteem, more honor, more dignity, and pride
We walked tall with our heads held high
And from ourselves there was no need to run or hide
When we had less we really had more
For we appreciated that which we had
We clung to our faith and held tight to hope
For these were the things that enabled us to cope
When we had less we really had more
For we depended wholeheartedly upon the good Lord
We called upon His name when times were good
And we called upon His name when times were hard
When We Had Less

Come Inside *Beverly Leonard*

What the Old Folks Use To Say

The old folks use to say a whole lot of things
Things that, when I was younger, I didn't comprehend or discern
But now that I have lived longer upon the Earth
These truths that they told, I have come to learn
Like, baby, just keep a' living and you'll find out
Just what life and living is all about
You may be up one day and then down tomorrow
Life's no easy journey, my child, they'd say
It's full of heartache, pain, trouble, sadness, and sorrow
But thank God that weeping lasts for only a night
Because joy comes in the morning, my child
And when tomorrow comes, everything is going to be all right
Because time heals all wounds, and this, too, shall pass
And nothing but the Word of the Lord
And what you do for Him is going to last
Just keep the faith, my child, they'd say
And don't let nobody turn you round
Turn you round, turn you round
Don't let nobody, child, turn you round
And remember, what goes around comes right back around
And what goes up, they'd say, must come down
They said that if you lie, you'll cheat and steal
So, do right, live right, love right, and obey God's holy will
Or upon the Earth your days will be numbered
Stay alert, they'd say, for many have fallen
While they slept and slumbered
And what's done in the dark shall surely come to the light
And two wrongs don't make a right
Besides, a hard head makes a soft behind
Seek ye God's Kingdom and God's Kingdom ye shall find
And remember, what you sow, you shall surely reap
They said that sometimes it's best to just let sleeping dogs sleep
But if you lie down with dogs, you'll get up with fleas
And when opportunities knock, opportunities we must seize
They said learn all that you can while you can
And always be willing to lend a helping hand

Come Inside   *Beverly Leonard*

They said be thankful, my child, for what you've got
Whether it be a little or whether it be a lot
They said that all that glitters is not gold
And that the grass is not always greener on the other side
And that from the Lord we cannot run or hide
And when you don't know which way to turn, my child
They said turn to the Lord in prayer
Now, He may not come just when you want him to come
But He's always right on time and He's always right there
Now, a house is not always a home, they'd say
But even if you live in a cave, you can still keep it clean
They said that when company comes
On your very best behavior you'd better be on
They said, under this roof, you'll obey and not do simply as you please
They said money doesn't come easy nor does it grow on trees
And where there's a will there's always a way
Try and try again they would always say
And from the straight and narrow path, they said we must not stray
They said don't burn your bridges or for others dig ditches
And don't think you're too big, my child, for your britches
And be careful, my child, of the company you keep
And of those in whom you befriend
For fair-weathered friends won't be there for you in the very end
They said you can't tell everyone your hopes, visions, and dreams
For everyone is not who they say they are or what they seem
And if you can't say nothing good about someone
Don't say anything at all
And the bigger they are the harder they'll fall
They said, baby learn your lessons and learn them well
Because, child, you don't want to end up in hell
So, put God first, my child, in all that you do
And everything else will be added unto you
Obey God's Word and in Him put all your faith and trust
Because He is a Way Maker and He still has great love for us
Yes, the old folks use to say a whole lot of things
Things that make a whole lot of good sense today
So, let us listen and heed the words of the old folks
Yes, let us listen to what the old folks have to say
What the Old Folks Use To Say

Come Inside *Beverly Leonard*

What Happened to the Village

Just the other day I drove a familiar way
And was drawn to a particular spot
It was the place where my life began so long ago
But all I found was an empty and deserted lot

The old brick wall that I use to climb
As well as the old oak trees
Stood not in their old yet familiar places
Only embedded within my memories

And the old frame house with the big, big porch
Was demolished and destroyed years ago
Now, weeds and trash take its place
The place where flowers use to grow

While standing in that empty lot my mind went back in time
To a place much different than the present
To a time when love and caring were, oh, so evident
To a time when family values, love, honor, and respect
Ran long and deep within the hearts of everyone you met

To a time when neighbors were truly kind and compassionate
And everyone did their neighborly part
To build, uplift, and encourage one another
To a time when sharing and caring came from the heart

For when one had, we all had
It was just the way things were done
And even though there were many of us
We really were just one

The teachers were genuine and they really and truly cared
They nurtured our potentials and our behinds they rarely spared
But the discipline didn't kill us, but it kept us on the narrow path
While molding fine morals, values, and characters that would last

Come Inside   *Beverly Leonard*

The churches were our meeting places
And Sunday school a must
For Christ was the head of our community
And the Bibles rarely ever collected dust

The grown-ups kept a watchful eye
On all the neighborhood kids
And if they saw you acting up in the neighborhood
You'd wish you never did

For when they were through chastising you
They would call your mom and dad
And they would be waiting with their belts
And give you more of what you just had

Then there were your grandparents
Who would give you the evil eye
And don't forget Aunt Jean and Uncle John
And older Cousin Di

They, too, would give you very good reasons
Why it was best just to be good
For the next time would be worst, they'd say
If you acted up in the neighborhood

Yes, life was good in my old neighborhood
For this was my village, my safe cocoon
It indeed took a village to help raise me
But my village was destroyed way too soon

What happened to my village
That was once, oh, so strong
What happened to the villagers
Tell me what went wrong

They said it was for the sake of progress
That my village had to be destroyed
But progress for whom and at whose expense
For this so-called progress has left a tremendous void

Come Inside *Beverly Leonard*

Now, the rustling of the trees brought my mind back to reality
The reality that must be confronted and faced
That my once safe village, the cocoon in which I grew
Can never ever be replaced

For times are, oh, so different now
Than the times we had back then
We lost that special spirit
When we moved out and they moved in

Now, who will help me raise my children
For the old saying still holds true
If takes a village to raise our children
Now, tell me, what am I suppose to do

I then understood how the Indians felt
About their sacred grounds
For even though changes occur to the land
Sweet and precious memories still abound

Now, with one last look I said good-bye
To old memories of old times as well as old friends
But I had a very strong and intense feeling
That I'd be drawn to this very same spot once again
What Happened to the Village

~ ~ ~

Common Cocoons

As she read the words the poet had written
A warm stream of tears flowed down her face
For the words of the poet took her back in time
To the village in which she was reared and raised
And though the tears flowed like the great River Nile
There appeared on her face a warm and tender smile
Common Cocoons

Come Inside   *Beverly Leonard*

Where Have All the Villagers Gone

Tell me, where have all the strong Black villagers gone
Where are the strong Black fathers and the strong Black mothers
Who worked together as one to create strong Black homes
Where have they gone

Where are the strong Black grandparents
Who helped rear and raise their grandchildren to love the Lord
Where are the strong Black aunts and uncles
Who always helped out when times got difficult and hard
Where have they gone

Where are the strong Black children who listened and obeyed
Who, on the straight and narrow path, walked and stayed
Where have they gone

Where are the strong Black neighbors
Who looked out for one another
Where are the strong Black sisters and the strong Black brothers
Where have they gone

Where are the strong Black teachers
And the strong Black preachers
Where are the strong Black elders and the strong Black leaders
Where have they gone

Where are the strong Black entrepreneurs
And the strong Black shop owners and keepers
Where are the strong Black bakers and barbers
As well as the Black beauticians and the Black street cleaners
Where have they gone

Where are the strong Black strangers you'd meet on the streets
Who were always nice, kind, and polite
Who, on crowded buses, would offer you their seats
Where have they gone

If by chance you happen to see them
Please tell them that it's time to come back home
Where Have All the Villagers Gone

I Need the Village

I need the village to help me raise my children
For I cannot raise my children alone
I need the village to help lead and guide my children
And help my children to be strong
Yes, I need the village to help me raise my children
For I cannot raise my children alone
I need the **teachers** to help educate and enlighten their minds
So that knowledge, wisdom, and understanding they can find
I need the teachers to help elevate and lift my children higher
To help quench their thirst for learning and to keep the flame afire
I need the **preachers** and the **Sunday school teachers**
To help instill within my children the powerful Word of the Lord
So that when temptations and peer pressures press down upon them
Deciding right from wrong won't be difficult, complicated, or hard
Yes, I need the preachers and the Sunday school teachers
To help instill within my children the powerful Word of the Lord
I need good **neighbors** to be my extended eyes and ears
To help look after and care for my children when I'm not around
For to know that my children are in good neighborly hands
Will cause peace of mind within my soul and spirit to abound
Yes, I need good neighbors to be my extended eyes and ears
To help look after and care for my children when I'm not around
I need the **grandparents**, the **aunts**, the **uncles**, and all of the **kin**
I need mentors, **volunteers**, and true and trusted **friends**
I need the **storeowners**, the **shopkeepers**, and the **street cleaners**
I need the **bakers**, the **barbers**, the **beauticians**, and the **morticians**
I need the **mail carriers**, the **police officers**, and the **librarians**
I need the **counselors**, the **coaches**, the **cooks**, and the **politicians**
I need the **doctors**, the **lawyers**, and the **social workers**
And sometimes I may even need the help of **strangers** on the street
For we never know when in the company of strangers
It's really angels that we meet
Yes, I need the village to help me raise my children
For I cannot raise my children alone
I need the village to help my children to be strong
For I cannot raise my children alone
I Need the Village

I Want My Village Back

I want my village back
The village that helped rear and raise me
Yes, I want back my once-strong and united Black community
When, as a people, we lived, learned, and truly loved one another
When we all struggled hard, but we all helped each other
When families were strong and unified
When the husbands were the heads
And the wives stood faithfully by their sides
And together, they taught, led, and their children they did guide
When parents weren't scared to spank their children's behinds
When neighbors were good and they looked out for one another
When we respected, cherished, and appreciated each other
When self-esteem, honor, and pride were high on the list
And our children weren't labeled 'disadvantaged' or 'at-risk'
When teachers could teach and children obeyed
When, in the neighborhood, Black leaders worked, lived, and stayed
When we walked by faith and all the time prayed
When going to Sunday school and Church was a must
And the Bibles never collected dirt or dust
When we owned our own businesses in our own neighborhoods
And money flowed between us and the economy was good
When we had high hopes and strong determination
When we thirsted for justice, equality, and education
When it was safe to walk up and down the streets
And pleasantries were spoken by everyone you'd meet
When we didn't have a problem with guns, gangs, and drugs
When we didn't have to fear low-down and dangerous thugs
When we weren't afraid to stand up and boldly speak out
When we weren't consumed with worry, stress, fear, and doubt
Now, the village is under seize from within and out
Black family life has been blown straight to hell
Our children are hitting the skids and are not faring well
The teachers can't teach and the children disobey
The strong Black leaders have all moved away
And the rest of the body is lost and has fallen astray
While the drug dealers push drugs in the village all day
Black people are strung out on crack cocaine
That demonic spirit that's driving our people completely insane

Come Inside *Beverly Leonard*

It's got us walking around looking like zombies without any brains
And the deadly disease called **AIDS** is now present and taking claims
And the shopkeepers don't look or speak like us anymore
And we don't call upon the good Lord like we did once before
It seems that when integration moved in
Our village exploded and eroded right to the very core
I want my village back like it was before
I Want My Village Back

~ ~ ~

Mr. Buddy's Razor Strap

Mr. Buddy was an elderly man
Who lived in the old neighborhood
Just as nice a fellow as he could be
But Mr. Buddy had a mean razor strap
That scared the daylights out of me
Now, I would often visit Mr. Buddy's house
For his children were very good friends of mine
We'd laugh, play ball, jacks, dolls, and house
But while inside, I was always quiet as a little mouse
For I had heard the stories of Mr. Buddy's razor strap
And it created great fear within my mind and heart
And the Lord knows that I would often shake and tremble
For Mr. Buddy's razor strap, I wanted no part
Now, Mr. Buddy never got me with that strap
For the fear of it kept me straight in line
But you could not have made me believe back then
That if needed, Mr. Buddy would not have whipped my behind
But looking back in time, I can now clearly see
That Mr. Buddy's razor strap represented
The strength of our once-strong Black community
Well, Mr. Buddy died many years ago
But I often wonder what happened to his razor strap
Thank you, Mr. Buddy, for helping to keep me in line
For the fear of it helped me to turn out just fine
Thank you, Mr. Buddy, for your razor strap
Mr. Buddy's Razor Strap

They Take Me Back

Some songs, some things, some places
And some old, yet, familiar faces sometimes take me back
They cause my mind to shift and jump off track
They take me back to by-gone days
When we lived, loved, and learned in different ways
Yes, they sometimes take me back to by-gone days
To days when life wasn't so overwhelmed
With great heartache, stress, and strife
When it seemed as if we placed greater value on the gift of life
When families were unified, fortified, and strong
To a time when parents taught their children right from wrong
And together they created for their children safe and happy homes
When fathers were the heads and the mothers stood by their sides
And together, they reared, raised, and trained their children
And together, their children, they nurtured, led, and they did guide
They take me back to a time when we had strong neighborhoods
When everyone worked together as one for everyone's good
And nothing negative was allowed into our neighborhoods
To a time when we had strong leaders who stood up and spoke out
To a time when we knew what hard work and dedication was all about
To a time when we thirsted for truth, justice, and liberty
When high goals and objectives were set, met, and achieved
When respect was expected, given, and received
To a times when, in ourselves and in one another we believed
They take me back to a time when the spirit of love was in the air
When people looked out for one another
And for one another we genuinely and truly cared
To a time when we called, leaned, and depended on the Lord
To a time when we kept the faith even when times were hard
Yes, some songs, some things, some places
And some old, yet, familiar faces sometimes take me back
They cause my mind to shift and jump off track
They Take Me Back

Come Inside　　　　　　　　　　　　　　*Beverly Leonard*

Dinnertime

There was a time some time ago
When to the dinner table family members would often go
To sit together, to eat together, to chit chat and talk
About the things that were on their minds
It was dinnertime
And all around the table everyone would sit
And with hands held and heads bowed low
Someone would pray
Thank you, Heavenly Father, for this food today
It was dinnertime
And after the prayer at the dinner table was said
It was time to break bread
Table manners were taught by the old to the young
And were expected to be used at the dinner table by everyone
It was dinnertime
A time to converse, to dialogue, and to communicate
About this, that, and/or the other
A time to laugh, smile, or just sit, eat, and listen
It was a time to get closer to each other
It was dinnertime
But now times have changed and dinnertimes are not the same
For the foundations of the home and the family structure
Have been discombobulated and rearranged
Tell me, what happened to dinnertimes
Well, come and take a walk with me through my God-given gift of poetry
And let us step outside of the box and see just what we can see
The dinner table now sits in the corner collecting old mail and dust
And, where, oh, where are the members of the family, yes, where are 'us'
We are running both here and there and everywhere
In a fast-paced world that's really going nowhere
Everyone on different pages like parallel lines
Too busy to come together as one to sit, chit-chat, and dine
Oh, listen, families of the world, to the words of the poet
For the Creator of the family arrangement says
Because these essential elements we now lack
"It's time to bring family dinnertimes back"
So, come let us sit together, eat together, and together let us chit-chat
Let us hold hands, bow our heads, and together let us pray and break bread

Come Inside   *Beverly Leonard*

And let's be nice, polite, and mannerable to one another
After all, we are family, and we are suppose to love each other
Now, this is not to say that it's going to be an easy thing to do
But let us plan in advance and do it one step at a time
In both your home and mine
Until we bring back dinnertime
Dinnertime

~ ~ ~

I'm Tired

I'm tired of seeing Black men pushing baskets and begging for handouts
I'm tired of Black people being consumed with fear, worry, and doubt
I'm tired of Black people living their lives in drug-induced fogs
I'm tired of Black people disrespecting one another
And calling each other 'niggas', 'fools', and 'dawgs'
I'm tired of Black men calling their Black women degrading names
I'm tired of Black women acting like the names they're called without shame
I'm tired of Black parents not raising their kids as they know they should
I'm tired of Black parents spoiling their children as if being spoiled is good
I'm tired of drug dealers pushing drugs into our once-strong neighborhoods
I'm tired of other races disrespecting and degrading Black people
I'm tired of Black people disrespecting and degrading themselves
I'm tired of Black people pretending to be crazy just to get that check
I'm tired of Black people who are just plain lazy and don't want to labor and work
I'm tired of Black children misbehaving and acting bad in school
I'm tired of their parents who won't discipline them and make them obey the rules
I'm tired of seeing Black women and men not loving one another and getting along
I'm tired of seeing Black families shattered and scattered that were once so strong
I'm tired of jail cells and prisons being Black people's 'home away from home'
I'm tired of Black men not taking the lead and being supportive and strong
I'm tired of Black people who prosper and excel, but fail to give back in return
I'm tired because the deadly dangers of Willie Lynch our people have yet to learn
Now, tell me, are you tired, too
Well, you ought to be
Now, what shall we do about these terrible atrocities
Because I'm tired
I'm Tired

Come Inside *Beverly Leonard*

Reclaiming Our Children

Sometimes we wait until it's too late
To teach, reach, train, and discipline our children well
And if in this important mission, we fall short and fail
Then we set our children up for sure disaster
And ultimately for the fiery flames of hell
Yes, sometimes we wait until it's too late
To teach, reach, train, and discipline our children well
But the time has come; in fact, the time is indeed past due
To gather our precious children back into the family fold
And despite what others may think, say, or do
Reclaiming our children should be our number one goal
Yes, the time has come to gather our children back into the fold
And even though it is long past due, it's better late than never
So, mothers and fathers, sisters and brothers, and kinfolk, too
Let us pull our families back together again and start anew
For our people have always known how to raise our children
For our family structure was strong back in Africa's land
Where honor and pride ran long and deep
And respect was expected, given, and received
Even from strangers we'd happen to meet on the streets
Yes, our people have always known quite naturally
Just how the family structure was meant to be
But now it seems as if we have lost our once-strong sanity
A direct ill effect of 400 plus years of bitter and brutal slavery
But through if all, and despite this negative mind-setting travesty
Within us stills dwells this child-rearing and raising ability
To teach, model, lead, and guide our children along life's way
To root them firmly in the life-saving Word of the Lord
So that their living won't be made extra difficult and rock-hard
Yes, this God-given natural ability still survives and thrives
And within our very essence is still very much alive
So, parents, for our children let us do what we know best
And the good Lord who loves His children will do the rest
Let us reclaim and gather back into the family fold
Our beautiful and precious daughters and sons
Thus says the Lord, and what the Lord says shall be done
Reclaiming Our Children

The Reconditioning Of Our Minds

When a once-strong and intelligent mind
Becomes conditioned, contaminated, tainted, and intertwined
With bitter, twisted, deceptive, cold, and calculated lies
The once-strong mind shall eventually lose over time
Its strength and its wisdom that it once proudly held inside
Away goes the precious memories of a once-strong nation
Away goes the knowledge of its once-strong and firm foundation
And what remains is a sad state of chaos, conflict, and frustration
And in order to bring salvation and hope to the once-strong mind
There has to be a reconditioning that takes place over time
Or in a sad state of confusion, the mind will continue to be
As it unknowingly holds on to its mindset of slave mentality
But in order for the once-strong mind to begin to see with clarity
There has to be a reconditioning of our once-strong minds
So that true freedom our people can once again find
As well as our once-strong self-esteem, dignity, honor, and pride
So, let the reconditioning of our minds begin today
Let the reconditioning of our minds begin without further delay
The Reconditioning Of Our Minds

~ ~ ~

It's Time to Fly

Wake up, my beautiful Black people, wake up
Wake up from your hellish and nightmarish sleep
For no longer can we afford to sit idly by
And watch our people and our future die
Wake up, my beautiful Black people, wake up
For it's time for our people to take wings and fly
Wake up now, my beautiful Black people
For it's time for our people to fly
It's Time to Fly

It's Clean up Time

It's time to clean up our confused and chaotic minds
And get rid of all the clutter that has built up over time
So that true freedom and knowledge of self our people can find
So, let us gather our disinfectants, our gloves, and our washrags
And also our brushes, our brooms, and our heavy-duty trash bags
For this will be more than just an ordinary chore
It will take hard work, dedication, diligence, and determination
And it may cause anger, frustration, irritation, and aggravation
But this task must be done, for there is too much at stake
So, we must do it swiftly but thoroughly before it is too late
So, let the clean up and the restoration of our minds begin
Beginning with the bitter and twisted lies that were designed
Specifically to destroy and devastate our once-strong minds
Let us trash the lie that we came from a wild and savage place
And also the one that said we came from a wild and savage race
Lies that created within us self-hatred, shame, and disgrace
That robbed us of our honor, our dignity, our self-esteem, and pride
Let us sweep up the negative and deadly effects of Willie Lynch
That seek to separate, break, sever, destroy, and divide
And from our minds, let us toss these negative elements outside
Let us cast out complacency, envy, disrespect, and jealousy
Let us wipe out ignorance, idleness, stupidity, and illiteracy
Let us erase any trace of the desire for mind-altering drugs
That turn our people into mindless and dangerous thugs
Now, we must realize that it took time to obliterate our minds
And that it's going to take time to build our minds up once again
But the important thing is for this process in our minds to begin
So, let us continue to clean and scrub our minds each and every day
Until all the devastation and decay are completely wiped away
Then let us plant seeds of wisdom, truth, and knowledge
Of who we are and to whom we belong
For, with this wisdom, truth, and knowledge firmly in place
There's no way we can err or ever go wrong
It's Clean up Time

Freedom Is a State Of Mind

We've been waiting for Mr. Charlie to free us for a very long time
Realizing not that freedom comes from within
Realizing not that freedom is a state of mind

It doesn't come with an apology or monetary reparation
It didn't come with the signing of the Emancipation Proclamation
It's not about the forty acres or a bunch of dirty old mules
It's how we view ourselves
Whether we think we are a great and grand people
Or merely a bunch of imbeciles, idiots, and crazy, lazy fools

Yes, slavery is a state of mind
And after 400 plus years of oppression, suffering, and pain
We must now break free from this horrible mental bind
For slavery was more than mere shackles, whips, and chains
For when the physical chains were removed
Within many of our people the slave mentality remained

We must change the ways that we think of ourselves
For how we view ourselves directly determines
If our people and our future shall survive or sink
So, if we are to experience what true freedom really means
We must first change the ways that we think

No longer can we believe the lies that were told
Lies that were created and designed to destroy our very souls
We now know that from greatness and grandeur our people came to be
For we were created by the Grand Master Creator
Who created us strong, proud, Black, blessed, and free

Yes, the Lord planted freedom within our strong Black minds
And it is this very same freedom that our people must find
It will not come from Mr. Charlie or from anyone or anything else
For we must find true freedom within ourselves
For freedom is a state of mind
Now, let the search begin
Freedom Is a State Of Mind

Come Inside   *Beverly Leonard*

As High As Its Women

It has been said that a people can rise only as high as it lifts its women
And, if this be so, then we need to pause for the cause and come to see
Just how our women are treated in society
Are they held in high esteem and greatly revered and respected
Do they sit in positions that are honorable, noble, fine, and majestic
Or are our women treated with great scorn and disrespect
Are they beaten, bashed, abused, and suffering from total neglect
Just how do we treat our women
We need only to look around and plainly see
Just how earthly women are treated in society
And if you look and listen with discerning eyes and ear
You'll hear their weeping and witness their long river of tears
For in our society today, honor and respect for the woman
For the Black woman in particular has been blown to hell away
For many Black woman and also young Black girls
Are disrespected, dishonored, and highly abused
They are overburdened, stressed-out, manipulated, and used
But we all must remember the original position of the Black woman
For it is one of honor, strength, courage, and faith in the good Lord
And we must do whatever it'll take to place her back on her throne
Or the lives of our people will continue to be difficult and hard
And to all the Black women and young Black girls
Though you are tired, weary, worn out, and weak
You must continue to keep your integrity and stand on your own feet
It is not the time to give up, give in, or give out
For this is not what the Black woman is all about
The Black woman is the true salt of the Earth without a doubt
So, Black men, love, honor, cherish, and respect your Black women
And Black children, you do exactly the same
And the love, honor, and respect that you bestow upon them
Will help lift them up and their crown of glory they shall reclaim
If a people can rise only as high as it lifts its women
Then let the rising of our Black women begin today without delay
Or from upon the Earth, our people shall be forever wiped away
And Black women all over the world
Remember to love, honor, and respect God, yourself, and others
And rekindle and reignite your love for your Black brothers
As High As Its Women

Come Inside *Beverly Leonard*

Black Women, Hold On

Black women, hold on and be strong
And don't you ever give up, give in, or give out
For giving up, throwing in the towel, and calling it quits
Is not what the Black woman is all about
We must always remember from whence we came
For our roots contain no disrespect, dishonor, disgrace, or shame
For we came from a people great, wise, and strong
Strong physically, mentally, and spiritually
And upon the good Lord, our people clung and held on
And the Lord gave unto the Black woman
Courage and strength enough to carry a nation
He blessed her with the power to sustain, persevere, and endure
For the Black woman is one of God's greatest creations
She is the proud Black mother, daughter, sister, cousin, and kin
She is the good neighbor, aunt, niece, stranger, and friend
She is the teacher, the preacher, the counselor, and the reacher
She encourages and inspires and she lifts others higher and higher
For the Black woman is the true salt of all the Earth
And it has been this way since the very beginning of Mankind's birth
So, Black women, please hear my humble and heartfelt call
The Lord knows that you've grown tired, weary, and weak
But the Lord says unto the Black women of the world
Be strong and hold on and stand firm in your faith and on your feet
For He who has brought you thus far shall continue to lead you on
He shall refreshen your tired, weak, and weary souls
He shall renew your strength like eagles and make you strong
Black women, the Lord says that you must continue to hold on
For our men have been beaten and bashed and treated like trash
Our children are running amok and are dying each and every day
Crack cocaine is driving our people completely insane
And from the good Lord our people have fallen astray
Therefore, my Black sisters, our God-given strength we must reclaim
We must help lift our Black men to their original positions
And our precious children we must teach, reach, raise, and train
And let us love and respect one another as true sisters in God's holy name
Black women, hold on and be strong
Black Women, Hold On

Come Inside   *Beverly Leonard*

Black Men, Where Are You

Black men, where are you
Though I search for you, you I cannot find
But I know that you exist
For I see the beautiful Black seeds you've left behind

Black men, where are you
For your women and your children
Are suffering and crying out in a loud and desperate plea
Saying, "Come home, my husband, my father, my beloved
Come home and return to your family"

Black men, where are you
I know that you've been dealt a very hard and heavy blow
For you've been beaten and bashed and treated like trash
Lynched, castrated, rejected, oppressed, humiliated, and hated
But through it all, oh, Black men, you must remember
That from greatness and glory you came to be
From a God who is omnipotent, almighty, powerful, and holy
Who, in Mother Africa, created the strong Black family

Black men, where are you
For you have only to look around and sadly see
The destruction and dysfunction of our once-strong Black family

Black men, where are you
For we need you now more that ever before
To lead, to guide, to protect, and to provide
We need you, oh, Black men, if our people are to survive

Come home, oh, Black men, come home
Come home where you rightfully belong
Return to your original position
As the head of the Black family
And we shall lovingly stand proudly by your side
And together, we shall forge forward with God as our guide
We anxiously await your glorious return
Come Home, Black Men, Come Home

A Circle of Beautiful Black Brothers

I beheld a circle of beautiful Black brothers today
And these are the words that quickly came my way
Strong
Black
Educated
Intelligent
Determined
Motivated
Dedicated
Devoted
Divine
And, oh, so fine
Truly one of a kind
It sent chills down my spine and made me feel so good inside
To see my beautiful Black brothers standing there with pride
Right on, my beautiful Black brothers, right on
You really blew my mind
A Circle of Beautiful Black Brothers

~ ~ ~

Together Again

It's time for the Black woman and for the Black man
To come back together in love and in unity once again
For, there once was a time when the love between the two
Was so beautiful, strong, steadfast, dedicated, and true
But because of a destructive and diabolical plan
To separate the Black woman from her Black man
The relationship between the two have been like sinking sand
But now it's time for the Black woman and for the Black man
To come back together in love and in unity once again
And, of this truth, the angels in the Heavens shouted
Amen, Amen, Amen
Together Again

Come Inside   *Beverly Leonard*

There's Got to Be a Better Way

There's got to be a better way
For Mankind to live together in peace upon this Earth
To live and to love and to get along with one another
To live and to love as true sisters and brothers
There's got to be a better way

There's got to be a better way
For my Black people to live each day
For, each day, my Black people struggle just to survive
Each day my Black people find it hard just to stay alive
There's got to be a better way

There's got to be a better way
For Black men and Black women to communicate and get along
For in order for our people and our future to survive
The Black man and the Black woman must hang together strong
There's got to be a better way

There's got to be a better way
To rear, raise, and train our children as we know we should
We must stop listening to others who have trouble with their own
And create for our children happy, safe, secure, and loving homes
There's got to be a better way

There's got to be a better way
To stop negative influences from infiltrating our neighborhoods
For there are guns, gangs, drugs, and low-down dirty thugs
Selfish for greedy gain causing nothing but heartache and pain
There's got to be a better way

There's got to be a better way
Wake up now, my people, and let us come together as one
Let us come together now before the setting of the sun
Let us come together with one purpose, one vision, and one mind
Under the grand leadership of the Creator of all Mankind
For then and only then true peace and joy we all shall find
For, there is no other way
There Is No Other Way

Into The Abyss

The human mind can become eroded over time
Eroded with lies and deceit designed to keep us off our feet
Eroded with low self-esteem, a lack of dignity, honor, and pride
Filled with shame and disgrace caused by the twisted lies
Eroded by a lack of respect for God, self, and others
While Willie Lynched into hating our sisters and our brothers
Eroded by a sense of inferiority and a sense of complacency
That has made us slothful, weak, lazy, and slightly crazy
Eroded by negative music and dance that keep us weighed down
For such a demented mentality keeps us pressed to the ground
Eroded by mind-altering drinks and dangerous drugs
That have turned us into dangerous criminals and mindless thugs
Eroded by a nation built on bigotry, hatred, and greed
Planned and programmed so that the Black man cannot succeed
But every good plan can go astray
And it's high time for this one to be blown straight to hell away
It is time, my people, to stop the erosion of our once-strong minds
For, then and only then can true freedom we all shall find
Therefore . . .
Into the abyss
We throw the **bitter and twisted lies** that were told
Lies created and designed to destroy our minds and souls
And onto the wonderful truths of who we are, we quickly grab a hold
Into the abyss
We throw **Willie Lynch** and his bag full of evil and divisive tricks
While reclaiming camaraderie, brotherhood, and unity
That we once had back then in our Black communities
Into the abyss
We throw **complacency, laziness, and lack of determination**
And come to realize that we are one of God's greatest creations
Into the abyss
We throw **negative music, dance, drinks, and drugs**
And act no longer as pigeons, castaways, or trifling scrubs
Into the abyss
Shall descend those who hate their fellow man
Because of the color of their beautiful Brown and Black skin
Yes, into the abyss these things shall be tossed
For, then and only then, can we reclaim those things that were lost
Into The Abyss

One, Two, Three

Okay, my beautiful Black people
When I count to three
No longer hypnotized and programmed our people shall be
When I count to three
When I count to three
We shall regain complete control
Over our once-strong and precious memory
When I count to three
When I count to three
No longer will we believe the bitter and twisted lies that were told
Lies created and designed to devastate and destroy our very souls
When I count to three
When I count to three
No longer will our people be divided, disunited, tattered, and torn
But we shall be reconnected, resurrected, rejuvenated, and reborn
When I count to three
When I count to three
The Willie Lynch syndrome, which separates and divides our people
Will finally come to an end
And down into the abyss of hell
This negative and deadly mindset shall fast and furiously descend
When I count to three
When I count to three
Our people shall regain the knowledge
Of who we are and to whom we belong
That we came from the great and grand Creator
Who, from His divine and perfect image
Created us proud, Black, intelligent, and strong
When I count to three
When I count to three
United as one people our people shall be
One
Two
Three
When I Count to Three

Shondo Means Hello

To my Black brothers and sisters scattered over land and sea
The Greatest Spirit on High says to listen to me
~
As we journey through life and our paths do cross
Let us no longer ignore, slight, and disregard one another
As if we have forgotten or could care less
That we're still true sisters and brothers
But with a spiritual eye and a nod of our heads
Without fear, apprehension, intimidation, and dread
But with respect and honor, let us acknowledge one another
For too long we have fought and struggled against each other
And because we are so divided, strewn about, tossed, and scattered
We desperately need to reunite as a People and come back together
So, this message goes out to all of my Black sisters and brothers
Because, whether we want to believe it or not, we need one another
So, like a gentle dove, this message goes out to help spread love
May it soar far and wide over land and sea both high and low
And to the four corners of the world may this message go
So that God's beautiful Black people will come to know
That amongst our people from this day forward

Shondo means Hello

May it be as glue that helps heals, builds, binds, and bonds
As it is firmly planted into the hearts, minds, and souls of everyone
Let the world know that **The Shondo Movement** has now begun
To reunite and fortify God's beautiful Black daughters and sons
Now, fly, gentle dove, fly with this message of unity and love
May it fall upon our people like sweet manna from Heaven above
Until all of our people around the world come to know that

Shondo means Hello

So, when our paths do cross down here below
We will greet one another with a warm and genuine **Shondo**
Now after this message, my sisters and brothers you read or hear
You, too, must help spread this message both far and near
Yes, tell everyone down here below that **Shondo means Hello**
Shondo Means Hello

Come Inside *Beverly Leonard*

Martin Was Our Moses

A Tribute to Rev. Dr. Martin Luther King, Jr.

January 15, 1929 - April 4, 1968

~

Martin was our Moses
Called by God to deliver his beautiful Black people
Up and out of the bondages of racism and bigotry
He stood up, spoke out, and peacefully fought against the terrible ills
Of segregation, discrimination, injustice, and inequality
Yes, this humble man of God heard the Lord's call
And through it all, Martin stood steadfast, unafraid, and tall
And though Martin, like Moses, didn't make it to the Promise Land
Like Moses, God allowed Martin on the mountaintop to stand
And though a sniper's bullet took our beloved Martin away
He left us a strong and proud legacy that still lives on today
A legacy that says, "We are all God's children
And we must learn to live together as brothers
Or we shall perish together as fools
For injustice anywhere is a threat to justice everywhere"
Martin said, "No, no, no, we will not be satisfied
Until justice rolls down like waters
And righteousness like a mighty stream"
Yes, Martin was our Moses
Martin was our king
Let freedom ring
Martin Was Our Moses

~ ~ ~

The Missing Link

If we don't make some drastic changes in the ways that we act and think
Then our people shall continue to collapse, plunge, submerge, and sink
Until, on the Human chain, our people shall become the missing link
If we don't make some drastic changes in the ways that we act and think
The Missing Link

"I will exalt you, my God the King.
I will praise your name forever and ever.
Every day I will praise you and extol your name forever and ever.
Great is the Lord and most worthy of praise.
His greatness no one can fathom."

Psalm 145: 1-3

Chapter Eight
Praise the Lord

Sing Praises to the Lord

Sing praises to the Lord, all ye nations
For to Him alone belongs the honor, the praise, and the glory
For the Lord is still on His holy and heavenly throne
He is still almighty, omnipotent, all-powerful, and strong
Sing praises to the Lord, all ye nations
Sing praises to the Lord, all ye nations
For He is Lord of Lords and King of Kings
He is Alpha and Omega, the Beginning and the End
And upon Him we can call, lean, trust, and depend
Sing praises to the Lord, all ye nations
Sing praises to the Lord, all ye nations
For, from His perfect and divine image, Mankind came to be
And because He has not forgotten that we came from dust
He still has great mercy, compassion, and love for us
Sing praises to the Lord, all ye nations
Sing praises to the Lord, all ye nations
For He loved and still loves the world so very much
So much so, that He sent His only begotten and beloved Son
As a perfect ransom sacrifice to save from sin the lives of everyone
Sing praises to the Lord, all ye nations
Sing praises to the Lord, all ye nations
For Jehovah has promised a glorious resurrection in the end
And if we abide in His holy and inspired Word
In Paradise with Him we shall eternally spend
Sing praises to the Lord, all ye nation
Sing praises to the Lord, all ye nation
For He is truly great and worthy to be praised
Sing Praises to the Lord

~ ~ ~

He Alone Is Worthy

He alone is worthy to be praised
So, let us give Him the honor and the glory all of our days
For He alone is worthy to be praised
He Alone Is Worthy

Oh, Come Let Us Worship the Lord

Oh, come let us worship the Lord
Let us humbly come before His holy presence
With thanksgiving, joy, praise, and love
Oh, come let us worship the Lord
Let us worship Him in truth and in spirit
For He is the Greatest Spirit of all
And unto His divine and holy name
We joyfully lift our voices and call
Oh, come let us worship the Lord
Let us sing, dance, and shout glory hallelujah
Let us exalt His holy and righteous name
Let us make a joyful noise before His heavenly throne
For to Him belongs the glory and to Him alone
Oh, come let us worship the Lord
Let us lift our hands way up high
And because we have all been blessed by His goodness
Of His goodness we all can bear witness and testify
Oh, come let us worship the Lord
For He has brought us all from a mighty long way
And because He has promised never to leave us alone
By His side, as our savior and guide, we long to forever stay
Oh, come let us worship the Lord
So that when His Son returns on that great day
We will be able to stand before His holy throne
And continue to worship and praise the Lord all day
Oh, Come Let Us Worship the Lord

~ ~ ~

I'm Not Ashamed

I'm not ashamed to lift God's holy and righteous name
Yes, when it comes to giving my Lord and Savior praise
For His goodness, His mercy, and His saving grace
I'm not ashamed
I'm Not Ashamed

Oh, What a Mighty God We Serve

Oh, what a mighty God we serve
Mighty in power, strength, and majesty
Mighty in mercy, grace, and glory
Mighty in wisdom and understanding beyond compare
Mighty in righteousness, truth, and being faithful and fair
Mighty in miracles and blessings that rain down from Heaven above
Mighty in compassion, kindness, and agape love
Mighty in giving and in the forgiving of our sins
And in Him we can always trust and depend
Oh, what a mighty God we serve
Oh, What A Mighty God We Serve

~ ~ ~

Let Us Worship the Lord Together

Oh, come let us worship the Lord together
Let us lift His holy name way up high
Let us sing, dance, and shout hallelujah
Let our voices in unison reach to the sky
For to Him belongs the honor
And to Him belongs the praise
So, come let us worship the Lord together
Yes, let us worship the Lord all of our days
Let Us Worship the Lord Together

~ ~ ~

Come, Taste, and See

Come, taste, and see just how good God is
See how He will lift, strengthen, sustain, and carry you safely through
See how He will rain His many and mighty blessings down upon you
Yes, come, taste, and see just what God can do
Come sit at His table of plenty and sup
And drink from His heavenly and holy cup
Come, taste, and see just how good God is
Come, Taste, and See

What God Is This

What God is this who created the Heavens and also the Earth
Through His infinite power, wisdom, understanding, and glory
Who stands alone, for there is no other like Him to be found
For He is magnificent, omnipotent, almighty, and holy

What God is this who created the sun to shine by day
And the moon and the stars to illuminate by night
Who set the patterns for the planets and the galaxies
To spin and rotate in their orbits just right

What God is this who created the great expanse
Which caused the waters above to separate from the waters below
Who gathered the seas together and lifted the dry land
Without lifting nary a finger or waving a hand

What God is this who supplied the entire Earth
With seed-bearing plants and fruit-yielding trees
Who filled the waters with every kind of living creature
Who filled the sky with winged birds and sweet bumblebees

What God is this who filled the Earth
With every living creature according to their very own kind
From livestock to creatures that move along the ground
And every species of wild animals upon the Earth you could find

What God is this who created Mankind
For, from His very own image, Mankind came to be
To rule over the Earth and all of its creatures
From the livestock and the birds to the fish of the sea

What God is this who made all things great and grand
Who made all things perfect, fine, and good
This God is truly awesome, all-powerful, majestic, and holy
And to Him alone belongs the praise, the honor, and the glory

He is the God of Abraham, Isaac, and Jacob
He is the Lord of Lords and the King of Kings
And to Him alone we lift our voices and sing
What God is this - He is the God I choose to serve
What God Is This

God Is Truly Awesome

God is truly awesome
More than mere words can possibly say
And I am so glad that He loves me as He does
In such an awesome agape kind of way
God is truly awesome

God is truly awesome
We need only to look at nature and plainly see
His great and grand love for all Mankind
And His great and grand love for diversity
God is truly awesome

God is truly awesome
And He is still on His heavenly and lofty throne
He is still almighty, omnipotent, all-powerful, and holy
He is still all merciful, forgiving, gracious, and strong
God is truly awesome

God is truly awesome
And He is still knocking at our door
He is still ready, willing, and surely able
To give us so much more
God is truly awesome

God is truly awesome
And to Him alone belongs the praise, the honor, and the glory
For He has promised eternal and everlasting life
He has promised to do away with pain, suffering, death, and strife
God is truly awesome

God is truly awesome
And we must come to know Him for ourselves
For His mercy, love, grace, and compassion for us
Cannot be compared to anything or anyone else
God is truly awesome

So, let us come to know the love of the Lord for ourselves
For the love of the Lord is truly awesome
God Is Truly Awesome

Rejoice Always

"Rejoice always," says the Lord
But how can I rejoice when times get so difficult and …
"Rejoice always," says the Lord
But how can I rejoice when troubles, trials, and tribulations …
"Rejoice always," says the Lord
But how can I rejoice when my bills pile high and my money is …
"Rejoice always," says the Lord
But how can I rejoice when I can't seem to make the two ends …
"Rejoice always," says the Lord
But how can I rejoice when I have so many hungry mouths to …
"Rejoice always," says the Lord
But how can I rejoice when I become frustrated, agitated, and …
"Rejoice always," says the Lord
But how can I rejoice when I try to do my best and my best isn't …
"Rejoice always," says the Lord
But how can I rejoice when I'm overwhelmed and burdened …
"Rejoice always," says the Lord
But how can I rejoice when others talk about me behind my …
"Rejoice always," says the Lord
But how can I rejoice when my name and reputation is under …
"Rejoice always," says the Lord
But how can I rejoice when I'm depressed, lonely, and …
"Rejoice always," says the Lord
But how can I rejoice when life tries to knock me off my …
"Rejoice always," says the Lord
But how can I rejoice when my spirit is tired, weary, and …
"Rejoice always," says the Lord
But how can I rejoice when my body aches and is in so much …
"Rejoice always," says the Lord
But how can I rejoice in times of chaos, conflict, and …
"Rejoice always," says the Lord
But how can I rejoice in times of regret, disappointment, and …
"Rejoice always," says the Lord
But how can I rejoice when I don't receive the love that I …
"Rejoice always," says the Lord
But how can I rejoice when my children act up and misbe- …
"Rejoice always," says the Lord

But how can I rejoice when death comes a' calling upon those ...
"Rejoice always," says the Lord
But how can I rejoice in a world filled with bigotry and ...
"Rejoice always," says the Lord
But how can I rejoice when there are wars and rumors of ...
"Rejoice always," says the Lord
But how can I ...
"Rejoice always," says the Lord
But ...
"Rejoice always," says the Lord
B ...
"Rejoice always," says the Lord
Rejoice Always

~ ~ ~

Shout

The reason why I can lift my hands up high
And shout **"Glory hallelujah"** and **"Thank you, Lord"**
Is because I've been through some storms in my life
And many have been quite difficult, stressful, and hard
Yes, I've been through some storms and back again
And because He's been with me through thick and through thin
I must give the praise, the honor, and the glory back to Him
For where, oh, where in the world would I be
If it had not been for God's goodness and His mighty mercy
So, if you see me lifting my hands up high
And shouting **"Glory hallelujah"** and **"Thank you, Lord"**
And you don't understand just where I'm coming from
Just keep a' living, my child, and this wisdom shall surely come
And then you shall understand just where I'm coming from
When I lift my hands up high
And shout, **"Glory hallelujah"** and **"Thank you, Lord"**
For you've been so good to me
"Glory hallelujah"
"Thank you, Lord"
Shout

Break Out In Praise

When troubles, trials and tribulations come your way
Break out in praise
When you're having a really hard and difficult day
Break out in praise
When others try to break and bring your good spirit down
Break out in praise
When it seems that peace of mind just can't be found
Break out in praise
When your bills pile high and your money is tight
Break out in praise
When nothing seems to be going right
Break out in praise
In times of worry, stress, and strain
Break out in praise
When you feel as if you're going completely insane
Break out in praise
When your body aches and you're in constant pain
Break out in praise
In times of suffering, sadness, heartache, and sorrow
Break out in praise
When you're down and out and can't visualize a brighter tomorrow
Break out in praise
In times of anger, hurt, frustration, and temptation
Break out in praise
In times of disappointment, despair, and desolation
Break out in praise
In times of happiness, joy, and jubilation
Break out in praise
And spite the devil
For, in times of praise, satan is completely powerless and shut down
he is rendered null and void and can't hang around
For he and his demons cannot operate on holy ground
And in times of praise much holiness is found
For, when praises go up, blessings come down
So, in times like these
Whether you stand up right or fall on your knees
In all of your days break out in praise
Break Out In Praise

Come Inside   *Beverly Leonard*

When I See These Things

When I see . . .

The glory of the sunrise in the early morning dawn
The splendor of the setting of the late evening sun
The beauty of the wildflowers that bloom in the early spring
The strength of an eagle's expanded and soaring wings
The breathtaking view of the Grand Canyon and the cascading falls
The majesty of the great sequoia trees standing steadfast and tall
The radiance of a colorful and vibrant rainbow
The marvel of childbirth and the soft and driven snow
The awesomeness of the oceans and the rivers that ebb and flow
The dynamic creatures that live in the watery depths below
The diversity of the fruits and vegetables that sprout and grow
The magnificence of the mountains that peak and reach way up high
The brilliance of the stars that twinkle and shine in the midnight sky
The power of earthquakes, tornadoes, and hurricanes
The might of mudslides, hailstorms, fire, wind, and rain
The exquisiteness of precious jewels, gems, and stones
The grandeur of the vast universe, which to Him belongs
The holiness of His Word that He so lovingly left behind
The power of the Holy Spirit in which great comfort we can find
The intelligence and the potential of the human mind
The genuine love that God has for all Mankind
The compassion that He shows us each and every day
How He blesses us and for us He always makes a way
When I see these things, they remind me that God is . . .
Glorious, Splendid, Beautiful
Strong, Breathtaking, Majestic
Radiant, Marvelous, Awesome
Dynamic, Diverse, Magnificent
Brilliant, Powerful, Mighty
Exquisite, Grand, Holy
Intelligent, Genuine, Loving
Compassionate, Giving, and a Way-Maker
When I see these things
When I See These Things

The Word of the Lord

The Word of the Lord is powerful, potent, and strong
The Word of the Lord will teach you right from wrong
The Word of the Lord motivates, encourages, and inspires
The Word of the Lord will never change or expire
The Word of the Lord nourishes, nurtures, and feeds
The Word of the Lord protects, guides, shields, and leads
The Word of the Lord comforts, counsels, and consoles
The Word of the Lord is complete, concise, and whole
The Word of the Lord connects our spirit with the Spirit of the Lord
The Word of the Lord strengthens us when times are difficult and hard
The Word of the Lord is a light that leads the way
The Word of the Lord keeps us from falling astray
The Word of the Lord is righteous, just, and true
The Word of the Lord will help lift us up and carry us through
The Word of the Lord has stood the test of time
The Word of the Lord is holy, inspired, sacred, and divine
The Word of the Lord will never return null or void
The Word of the Lord will never die or be destroyed
The Word of the Lord

~ ~ ~

The Word of God Is Alive

Apostle Paul declared that the Word of God is alive
And exerts power and is sharper than any two-edged sword
And pierces even to the dividing of soul and spirit
And of joints and their marrow
And is able to discern thoughts and intentions of the heart
Enough said
The Word of God Is Alive

Heb. 4:12

Know the Word

We must know the Word in order to use the Word
To fight satan with the Word
The mighty and powerful Word of the Lord
The Word that strengthens, reinforces, edifies, and fortifies us
In both good times and when times are difficult, stressful, and hard
The Word that liberates, sets free, leads, guides, and saves
The Word that makes satan and his demons obey and behave

Remember when Jesus was tempted by the devil in the wilderness
A part of that conversation went something like this:

satan said:	"If you are the Son of God, tell this stone to become bread"
Jesus replied:	***It is written:*** Man shall not live by bread alone, but by every word of God" **(Deut. 8:3)**

satan said:	"I will give you all the kingdoms of the world if you bow down and worship me"
Jesus replied:	***It is written:*** Worship the Lord your God and serve Him only" **(Deut. 6:13)**

satan said:	"If you are the Son of God, throw yourself down from here"
Jesus replied:	***It is written:*** "Do not put the Lord your God to the test" **(Deut. 6:16)**

Yes, each time satan tried to tempt Jesus
Jesus used the Word of God to fight the devil off
And just as Jesus used the Word, we, too, must use the Word
But how can we use the Word in times like these
If we don't know the Word of God with familiarity and ease
That is why it is essential that we come to know God's Word
And to plant His Word firmly in our minds and in our hearts
So that when, not if, but when satan attacks
Like Jesus, we can say to this manslayer
"Get thee behind me, satan, get back"
Know the Word

Soul Food

Just as we need to feed our minds and our bodies
We must also remember to feed our souls as well
For, if left unnurtured, untended, and unfed
Our souls will become bitter, brittle, and barren, as if dead
So, it is essential, you see, that our souls be well fed
So, let the grand and royal feast begin
Let there be a great gathering of the nations of earthly men
Let us gather together at the Human family table
Let us feed on God's Holy Word until we are no longer able
And like sweet manna falling from Heaven above
Let us joyfully partake of His powerful Word
And come to know of His goodness, His mercy, and of His love
Let us seek and find the Word
Let us study, learn, and discern the Word
Let us heed and obey the Word
Let us live and love the Word
Let us sense and feel the Word
Let us become consumed by the Word
Let us share and spread the Word
Let us keep our minds stayed on the Word
The mighty, mighty, mighty Word of the Lord
And if we do these things, our souls will become full
And in the end, we shall receive our heavenly reward
So, let us continue to feed our minds and our bodies as well
But let us also remember to feed and nourish our souls
To prevent our souls from spending eternity in hell
Soul Food

~ ~ ~

Our Walk with God

My walk with God is a very personal one
And on my walk with Him no one else can come
For my walk with God is a very personal one
And your walk with God is a very personal one, too
And no one can come along on God's walk with you
Our Walk with God

Believe

Believe in Jehovah
Believe that He is the One and Only True and Living God
And that besides Him, there is no other
Believe that He created the Heavens and also the Earth
Believe that unto Mankind and every living thing He gave birth
Believe that He loved the world so much that He gave His only Son
To save from sin and death the lives of everyone
Believe that Jesus Christ is God's only begotten Son
And that, to get to the Father, you must go through this holy One
Believe that Jesus died for our sins and rose on the third day
Believe that He is the Truth, the Life, the Light, and the only Way
Believe in God's holy and inspired Word that He lovingly left behind
So that truth, wisdom, hope, and salvation we all can find
Believe that God sent his Holy Spirit down when Jesus went away
Which teaches, leads, guides, comforts, and consoles us to this very day
Believe that God still cares so much about me and you
Believe that He knows just what we're all going through
Believe that He is still on His majestic and mighty throne
Believe that He is still all-powerful, omnipotent, and strong
Believe that He is still The Way-Maker
And that miracles He still performs
Believe that He will strengthen and fortify you
Believe that He will be with you in the midst of the storms
Believe that He will never leave you alone
Believe that He will lift you up and make you strong
Believe that God's Kingdom shall one day come
Believe that we all shall be judged by Jesus, His beloved Son
Believe in God's promise of everlasting life
Believe in a place called Paradise
Believe in spirit and believe in truth
For there is no other way
So, believe these things today
Believe

Come Inside *Beverly Leonard*

Imagine a World

Imagine a world . . .
Where people are not judged by the color of their skin
But by the content of their character that is found deep within
Imagine a world . . .
Where there are no injustices, inequalities, or discriminations
But a world that is honest and righteous in all human relations
Imagine a world . . .
Without warfare, violence, crime, or strife
Where peace and tranquility are the normal ways of life
Imagine a world . . .
Where there is no hunger, famine, thirst, or starvation
Where food and water are in abundance to feed the entire nations
Imagine a world . . .
Where there is no envy, jealousy, disdain, or discord
Where the people live in harmony on the same harmonious accord
Imagine a world . . .
Where there are no separations, divorces, or broken homes
Where love, honor, and respect run long, deep, and strong
Imagine a world . . .
Where money will not determine one's happiness or peace of mind
A world without bills, rent, taxes, and other outrageous fines
Imagine a world . . .
That is free of land, air, water, and mental pollutions
Where people come together as one to create positive solutions
Imagine a world . . .
Where there are no man-made calamities or natural disasters
Where the only loud sounds will be those of praise and laughter
Imagine a world . . .
Without language barriers that break down communication
But a world with one pure language which unites the nations
Imagine a world . . .
Where death, disease, and afflictions shall be things of the past
Where long life, good health, and happiness will forever last
Imagine a world . . .
Where there is love and respect for God, self, and others
Where everyone realizes that we're all true sisters and brothers
Now, imagine yourself living in this world
Imagine a World

A Place Called Heaven

I've heard of a place called Heaven
A place where peaceful and gentle waters flow
A place where the streets are paved with silver and gold
A place where I would love to one day go

I've heard of a place called Heaven
Where God sits on His heavenly and holy throne
And the angels sing praises to His holy name
For He is still almighty, omnipotent, all-powerful, and strong

I've heard of a place called Heaven
A place where the spirits of our dearly departed go
For our spirits return to the Giver and the Receiver of life
Leaving behind our physical and earthly shells below

I've heard of a place called Heaven
Where the Lord's holy light shines brilliant and bright
A place of true peace, joy, and serenity
A place filled with happiness, bliss, and total tranquility

I've heard of a place called Heaven
A kingdom both great and grand
And the Bible says that His Kingdom shall surely come one day
Yes, upon the Earth, God's Kingdom shall one day stand

And I hope and I pray that I'll be able to stand on that great day
When the Lord calls me before His heavenly and holy throne
I pray that I will have loved more than enough
To cover my sins and all of my wrongs

Yes, I've heard of a place called Heaven
And I pray that one day Heaven will be my home
A Place Called Heaven

A Peek into Paradise

The Lord allowed me a peek into Paradise
And these are the things that I, in awe, beheld that day
~
Streets made of precious gems, jewels, silver, and gold
Blissful and happy reunited spiritual souls
Shouting glory hallelujah all around God's heavenly throne
Throngs of angels singing holy, holy, holy
And praising the Lord all the day long
And peace, tranquility, and serenity flourished and abound
And joy, jubilation, and laughter were heard all around
It was pain, problem, tribulation, and trouble free
Immersed in truth, justice, love, life, and liberty
There were beautiful mansions with rooms galore
Each one more beautiful than the room before
And the light, oh, the light
How it shone so brilliantly and bright
And the glory and majesty of the Lord
Oh, what a wondrous and awesome sight
Yes, these are the things that I beheld that day
When the Lord allowed me a peek into Paradise
A Peek into Paradise

~ ~ ~

God Has Not Forgotten

God has not forgotten that we came from dust
And that is why He has great love, mercy, and compassion for us
Because He has not forgotten that we came from dust
This is what it says in God's holy and inspired Word
That lifts, leads, guides, and has the power to deliver us
Yes, it says that God has not forgotten that we came from dust
And that He still has great love, mercy, and compassion for us
Thank you, oh, Lord, for not forgetting that we came from dust
God Has Not Forgotten

When I Get To Heaven

When I get to Heaven
Oh, what a glorious time it shall be
For the sorrows of this old world will fade from my memory
Yes, when I get to Heaven, oh, what a glorious time it shall be

When I get to Heaven
I will see and feel the warm and wondrous light
The light that forever shines so brilliantly and bright
Yes, when I get to Heaven, I will see and feel the warm and wondrous light

When I get to Heaven
The beauty of God's Kingdom I will behold
I shall walk down the pearly streets of old that are paved with gold
Yes, when I get to Heaven, the beauty of God's Kingdom I will behold

When I get to Heaven
I'll be reunited with my family and friends
And our joyous celebration will never cease or come to an end
Yes, when I get to Heaven, I'll be reunited with my family and friends

When I get to Heaven
I shall find my very own special room
For Jesus said He'd go and prepare a place for me and shall return soon
Yes, when I get to Heaven, I shall find my very own special room

When I get to Heaven
I shall meet and greet God's only begotten and beloved Son
Who gave His life as a ransom sacrifice to save the lives of everyone
Yes, when I get to Heaven, I shall meet and greet God's beloved Son

When I get to Heaven
I shall stand before God's holy and righteous throne
And, with the angels, I will sing praises to the Lord all the day long
Yes, when I get to Heaven, I shall stand before God's holy throne
When I Get To Heaven

Come Inside   Beverly Leonard

The Bright Side

A poet once wrote these words:
*"There's a bright side somewhere
Yes, there's a bright side somewhere
So, don't you stop until you get there
For there's a bright side somewhere"*
~
Tell me where, oh, where is the bright side

The bright side is where our Heavenly Father resides
Where our Lord and Savior Jesus Christ
Sits proudly in glory at His Father's right side
This is the bright side

Where the angels of the Lord sing glory hallelujah
All around God's holy and righteous throne
Singing holy, holy, holy and praising the Lord all the day long
For He is still almighty, omnipotent, all-powerful, and strong
This is the bright side

Where love, peace, joy, and happiness reside
And the streets are paved with silver and gold
And other precious jewels and gems simply exquisite to behold
Where there are beautiful mansions and rooms galore
Each one more beautiful than the one before
This is the bright side

Where there is no darkness, dusk, gloom, or night
Only God's radiant, brilliant, and glorious light
That shines all around from day to day
And its brilliance shall never cease or go away
This is the bright side

Where the spirits of our dearly departed reside
Whom I hope and pray to see one day
If by God's mercy and grace
I make it to the bright side
This is the bright side
The Bright Side

At The Threshold of Eternity

As I stand at the threshold of eternity
Faith, Hope, and Love are present and are here with me
For they were my constant companions and friends
Throughout my earthly journey
But now the time has come to bid them each farewell and good-bye
For a different journey for me is near and nigh

So, good-bye, Faith
You were my anchor when the storms of life raged on
You were my pillar, my support, and the posts that I leaned on
And without you, oh, Faith, I could not have made it on through
But you have served your purpose well, my dear friend
Now I can move forward without you
Good-bye, Faith

Good-bye, Hope
You were the light that shone when darkness was all around
You kept my feet firmly planted on firm and solid ground
Without you, oh, Hope, I would not have been able to cope
But now, my friend, I can move on without you
For that which I hoped for has now become true
Good-bye, Hope

Now, Love, Love, Love
Where, oh, where would I be without you
One thing is for sure, and that is I certainly wouldn't be here
Standing at the threshold of eternity
For you, oh, Love, covered a multitude of my sins and iniquities
And because you are the true essence of life itself
I'm taking you, oh, Love, along with me
Now, together, let us cross the threshold of eternity
At The Threshold of Eternity

Come Inside   *Beverly Leonard*

Who Is This Jesus

Who is this Jesus
Who was sent from Heaven above down to the Earth
Who is this Jesus
Who was born of a virgin from an immaculate birth
Who is this Jesus
Who is so full of love, wisdom, mercy, grace, and glory
Who is this Jesus
Who is almighty, omnipotent, all-powerful, and holy
Who is this Jesus
Who was baptized by John
Who is this Jesus
Whom God proudly declared, "This is my Beloved Son"
Who is this Jesus
Who made satan's temptations null, void, and hollow
Who is this Jesus
Whom the disciples left their families and homes to follow
Who is this Jesus
Who turned water into wine
Who is this Jesus
Who healed the sick and restored sight to the blind
Who is this Jesus
Who raised the dead and caused the lame to walk
Who is this Jesus
Who expelled demons and made the dumb to talk
Who is this Jesus
Who spoke with great wisdom, insight, and authority
Who is this Jesus
Who walked on water, rebuked the wind, and calmed the raging sea
Who is this Jesus
Who fed 5000 with two fish and five loaves
Who is this Jesus
Who, of his own death and resurrection, forecasted and foretold
Who is this Jesus
Who drove the traders from the temple away
Who is this Jesus
Who taught his disciples how to pray
Who is this Jesus
Who is called The Truth, The Life, the Light, and The Way

Who is this Jesus
Who said, "Let the children come unto me"
Who is this Jesus
Whose yoke is refreshing, light, and made easy
Who is this Jesus
Who knelt down and washed his apostles' feet
Who is this Jesus
Who, at the last supper, broke bread, and with them did eat
Who is this Jesus
Whom Judas betrayed for 30 silver coins
Who is this Jesus
Who, three times, Peter denied even knowing
Who is this Jesus
Who was found faultless, flawless, and blemish free
Who is this Jesus
Who was crucified on a cross on Calvary
Who is this Jesus
Who rose from the grave on the third day
Who is this Jesus
Who can wash all of our sins away
Who is this Jesus
Who now sits in glory at his Father's right side
Who is this Jesus
Who shall return in glory to judge all Mankind
Who is this Jesus
Who Is This Jesus

~ ~ ~

Fear God

Why fear man when man can only destroy the body
But cannot destroy the soul
We should fear God instead
Who can destroy both the body and the soul
Then restore them both and make them whole
Fear God

I Bless You, Oh, Lord

I bless you, oh, Lord
For you have been mighty good to me
And without you in my life, oh, Lord
I don't know where in the world I would be
So, I bless you, oh, Lord
For you have been mighty good to me
I bless you in the morning
And I bless you throughout the day
I bless you when I lay down to sleep
I bless you Lord forever and always
I Bless You, Oh, Lord

~ ~ ~

Please Bless Me, Oh, Lord

Please bless me, oh, Lord, this I pray
For I need another blessing from you, oh, Lord, today
Please lead me, guide me, and show me the proper way
Please bless me, oh, Lord, with whatever I may need
To prosper, endure, excel, soar, achieve, and succeed
Please bless me also, oh, Lord, to be a blessing to others
Yes, please bless me to help up-lift my sisters and brothers
Please Bless Me, Oh, Lord

~ ~ ~

Satisfaction Guaranteed

Satisfaction guaranteed
If in God's Holy Word, you trust, abide in, and believe
For in His inspired and holy Word, true joy and peace can be found
Joy and peace the world cannot give nor can it take away
Therefore, if you seek real and lasting satisfaction
Then open up your heart and let Jesus in today
Satisfaction Guaranteed

Come Inside   *Beverly Leonard*

The You in Me

mUe

It's the You in me, oh, Lord
That causes me to rejoice, celebrate, and smile
It's the You in me, oh, Lord,
That makes me want to walk those extra miles
It's the You in me, oh, Lord
That makes me want to run on anyhow
It's the You in me, oh, Lord
that fills my heart with peace, gladness, and joy
It's the You in me, oh, Lord
That the world cannot take away or destroy
It's the You in me, oh, Lord
that makes me want to sing, dance, and shout
It's the You in me, oh, Lord
That chases away my fears, worries, dreads, and doubts
It's the You in me, oh, Lord
that strengthens me when I'm down and out
It's the You in me, oh, Lord
that brings comfort and solace to my soul
It's the You in me, oh, Lord
that makes me complete, full, and whole
It's the You in me, oh, Lord
that encourages and enables me to go on
It's the You in me, oh, Lord
that lifts me up, inspires me, and makes me strong
It's the You in me, oh, Lord
That consoles me in times of sadness and sorrow
It's the You in me, oh, Lord
that gives me hope for a better and brighter tomorrow
It's the You in me, oh, Lord
that loves to dwell on your holy and inspired word
It's the You in me, oh, Lord
That makes me walk a different walk and talk a different talk
It's the You in me, oh, Lord
That causes me to hold my tongue

Come Inside   *Beverly Leonard*

It's the You in me, oh, Lord
That prays for peace and for the salvation of everyone
It's the You in me, oh, Lord
That causes me to be merciful and compassionate to my fellow man
It's the You in me, oh, Lord
That makes me lend a helping hand
It's the You in me, oh, Lord
That causes me to love my enemies and them to forgive
It's the You in me, oh, Lord
That desires by thy side to always and forever live
It's the You in me, oh, Lord
It's the You in me
The You In Me

~ ~ ~

Between Me and the Lord

When I go to the House of the Lord to worship Him
It's between me and the Lord and no one else

When I lift my hands up high and shout glory hallelujah
It's between me and the Lord and no one else

When I stand before the altar and lay my burdens down
It's between me and the Lord and no one else

When I kneel down and pray at the end of the day
It's between me and the Lord and no one else

And when I'm called before the Lord's holy throne
It will be between me and the Lord and no one else
Between Me and the Lord

You Know the Lord Is Coming

You know the Lord is coming
You know He's on His way
When you look up and see the clouds overhead
You'll know that it's the Lord's Day
Yes, you'll know that it's Judgment Day
You know the Lord is coming
You know the Lord is coming
He's coming to judge us one and all
According to our deeds done upon the Earth
Some will live forever while others will surely fall
Listen to these words, my people, and heed this call
You know the Lord is coming
You know the Lord is coming
You know the Earth will rock, tremble, and shake
You know that some shall be saved on that great day
While others will be thrown into the fiery lake
Wake up now, my people, wake up, for too much is at stake
You know the Lord is coming
You know the Lord is coming
For the Earth has grown putrid and rotten to the very core
It must be as it was back then before the floodwaters came
When the Lord Himself shut the Ark's great and powerful door
Next time, He said, it will be fire instead
And not water like it was before
You know the Lord is coming
You know the Lord is coming
And He's coming with a vengeance of wrath, anger, and rage
He's coming soon to set matters straight
So, if you're not living your life as you know you should
You'd better change your life now before it is too late
You know the Lord is coming
You know the Lord is coming
You know He's on His way
When you look up and see the clouds overhead
You'll know that it's the Lord's Day
Yes, you'll know that it's Judgment Day
You Know the Lord Is Coming

Come Inside *Beverly Leonard*

Where Are You Trying To Go

Where are you trying to go - to Heaven or to Hell
For by your words, your deeds, and your actions, it's easy to tell
Where are you trying to go - to Heaven or to Hell

Are you loving one another and trying to be good
Are you obeying the Lord's Holy Word
And living your life as you know you should
Where are you trying to go - to Heaven or to Hell
For by your words, your deeds, and your actions, it's easy to tell

Are you filled with hatred, anger, envy, and greed
Is bitterness and contempt what you cultivate and breed
Do you dig ditches hoping that others will fall in
Is your life and your living consumed with worldly acts of sin
Where are you trying to go - to Heaven or to Hell
For by your words, your deeds, and your actions, it's easy to tell

Now, while there is still yet time, you'd better make up your mind
As to where you want your next journey to begin
Once your earthly journey down here ceases and comes to an end
For, if the road that you're on doesn't lead straight to the Lord
Then into the abyss your spirit shall eventually descend

For the Lord shall soon return to judge us one and all
According to our words, deeds, and actions done on the Earth
Many shall fall on Judgment Day
But there will be those who shall experience a glorious rebirth

Where are you trying to go - to Heaven or to Hell
For, by your words, your deeds, and your actions, it's easy to tell
Where are you trying to go – to Heaven or to Hell
Where Are You Trying To Go

Excuses

My hair is not fixed and I have absolutely nothing to wear
There's a hole in my stockings, and in my dress, there is a tear
I don't have a way to get to church because my car broke down
I have a hangover from last night and my head is spinning around
I must cook my Sunday meal, and I can't cook it if off to church I go
Besides, the Word of the Lord I already understand and know
I don't have to go to church because I have God in my heart
It's late and I'd rather not go if I'm not there from the very start
I don't have any money to put in the offering plate
I'll go once I work my problems out and get my life straight
My cat pooped in the living room and my dog ran away
I've got to wash my clothes and clean my house today
Oh, I'll just go another day
Yes, satan, the original liar, gives us many excuses to hinder us
From forming a close and personal relationship with the Lord
For anything that God is for, this manslayer is against
And the fellowshipping of God's people, he has a big problem with
But let us no longer be deceived or in his lies and excuses believe
For this traitor, this hater, this master-manipulator
Desires that all Mankind join him in the eternal fire
When God shall rid the world once and for all of this original liar
But until then, when Sunday mornings rolls around
You can bet that satan will be right there on the spot
For he wants us to join him in the place that is eternally hot
Yes, on Sunday mornings, satan works overtime
With the excuses, the false justifications, and all of the lying
But let us listen not to this evil and deceitful one
For soon his tragic and terrible end shall surely come
So, when Sunday morning comes back around
In the temples, synagogues, mosques, basilicas, or churches
We all should be found
Moreover, it says in the Word that when Jesus traveled all around
On Sundays, in the synagogue He could always be found
So, if it was good for Jesus to do, it's good for us, too
Now, let's get up and go give the Lord some praise
Yes, let us worship together in unison all of our days
No More Excuses

Come Inside   *Beverly Leonard*

Jesus Is Coming

Jesus is coming just as He said He would
Like a thief in the night, He will suddenly appear in sight
He'll return in the same fashion and in the same glorious way
He'll return with the clouds like the one that took Him up that day
And, upon His return, will you be filled with great joy and happiness
Or will His return cause you great fear, dread, and total distress
For every eye shall behold His magnificent face
And every knee shall surely bend
As the Lord of the high Heavens
From the high Heavens down to the Earth D
                                                                           E
                                                                           S
                                                                           C
                                                                           E
                                                                           N
                                                                           D
                                                                           S
Jesus Is Coming

~ ~ ~

You Don't Want To Be Left Behind

You don't want to be left behind
Because if you think the world is in bad shape now
Just wait until the saints vanish and are raptured away
When only sinners and evildoers shall be left behind
Those, who, from the good Lord did stumble and stray
Woe to the Earth on that dreadful day
When the great tribulation shall begin
Bringing desolation and devastation upon earthly man
Oh, what hard times these times shall surely be
So much pain, pestilence, heartache, hunger, and misery
No, you don't want to be left behind
For, if left behind, only doom and despair you shall surely find
You don't want to be left behind
You Don't Want To Be Left Behind

Last Words

These last words
Just like birds
Desired to be released and set free from their gilded and golden cages
They have been anxiously waiting and wishing to soar far over land and sea
To help spread the Good News of God's Kingdom through poetry
So, the poet releases these last words just like birds
Now fly, oh, words, fly as far as you possibly can
And deliver these last words to earthly man
Fly, last words, fly
Last Words

Chapter Nine
Last Words

God Is Still In Control

When hard times come like they always do
Remember, God is still in control
When those you depend upon turn their backs on you
Remember, God is still in control
When the storms of life rant and rage and the dark billows roll
Remember, God is still in control
When your bills pile high and your money is low
Remember, God is still in control
When you don't know which way to turn or which way to go
Remember, God is still in control
When it's hard to put food on your table
Remember, God is still in control
When you try to make the two ends meet, but you're just unable
Remember, God is still in control
When others talk about you behind your back
Remember, God is still in control
When your character and your reputation are both under attack
Remember, God is still in control
When others lie about you and slander your name
Remember, God is still in control
When others disappoint you time and time again
Remember, God is still in control
When you fail to receive mercy and compassion from your fellow man
Remember, God is still in control
When sadness and sorrow come your way
Remember, God is still in control
When it seems you just can't make it through another day
Remember, God is still in control
When your body aches and you're in so much pain
Remember, God is still in control
When it seems that you're going completely insane
Remember, God is still in control
When you hear of wars and rumors of wars
Remember, God is still in control
Now, bless your soul
And be glad that God is still in control
God Is Still In Control

Come Inside   *Beverly Leonard*

The Whole Duty of Man

King Solomon was a very wise and intelligent man
And a great leader and master teacher also was he
For God found favor in him and blessed him with insight and clarity
Yes, King Solomon sought true wisdom and true wisdom he did find
And he used his God-given gifts to lead and teach Mankind
And near the end of his earthly days
King Solomon concluded about life and learning this way
And to all that have ears
Please listen to what this wise man did say
For his words still hold true to this very day
So, listen with discernment to what this wise man did say
His conclusion went this way:

Fear God and keep His commandments
For this is the whole duty of man
For God will bring every deed into judgment
Both the good and the bad
And before His holy throne, we all shall be called to stand

So, let us heed these words of wisdom that were written long ago
By a man highly favored and blessed by God who was in the know
Let us fear God and His commandments let us always keep
So that in the end, blessed benefits we shall harvest and reap
Let us fear God and His commandments let us keep
For this is the whole duty of man
The Whole Duty of Man.

As We Go Along

I was taught in the kitchen when I was young
That it's best to clean up the mess as I go along
That way, my mother explained, in the end
A long time in the kitchen cleaning, I wouldn't have to spend
If I clean my mess as I go along
And just as surely as we live our lives upon the Earth
We must clean up our messes as we go along in life
For if we wait until the very end
To try to clean up our big pile of sin
Where, oh, where shall our souls descend
If we wait to clean up our messes at the very end
And remember, love covers a multitude of sins
So, let us be sure to love a whole lot
Let us give it all that we've got, so that in the very end
With the Lord in Paradise we shall forever spend
As We Go Along

~ ~ ~

The Bottom Line

The bottom line is that God created life
And that He created life so abundantly
He created the Heavens and He created the Earth
He created the plants, the animals, and the deep blue sea
He created you and He created me to live forever eternally
But sin entered in and now life is filled with great pain and misery
But because of God's great agape love and mercy for all Mankind
Tender mercy, grace, and forgiveness of our sins we all can find
A love so great that He sent His only begotten and beloved Son
Down to the Earth to save from sin and death the lives of everyone
He came to deliver a message from His Heavenly Father above
A message filled with hope, joy, peace, everlasting life, and love
Yes, He sent His only begotten Son to die so that we may live
And to those who endure until the very end
Eternal life-ever-after He promises to give
And that's the bottom line
The Bottom Line

If You Were To Die Today

If you were to die today
What would the Lord find in your heart
Would He find a lot of love, compassion, mercy, and grace
Or would He find a great deal of envy, jealousy, pride, and greed
Mixed with bigotry, bitterness, and hatred against another race
What would the Lord find in your heart if you were to die today
For what the Lord finds in your heart on that great day
Will directly affect where your soul will forever stay
If love, compassion, mercy, and grace unto others you did give
Then with the Lord in Paradise you will forever live
If the Lord finds in your heart much hatred, repugnance, and disdain
And a lack of love and compassion toward your fellow man
Then, before His holy throne, you will be unable to stand
And smack into the hellfires your soul shall land
If you were to die today
What would the Lord find in your heart
If You Were To Die Today

~ ~ ~

As If It Is Your Last Day

Live and love as if it is your last day
Give and forgive as if it is your last day
Care and share as if it is your last day
Show mercy and compassion as if it is your last day
Help and enhance Mankind as if it is your last day
Teach and reach others as if it is your last day
Study, learn, and discern as if it is your last day
Encourage and inspire others as if it is your last day
Pray and praise God as if it is your last day
Seek, ye, the Kingdom of Heaven as if it is your last day
Rejoice and celebrate life as if it is your last day
Get your house in order as if it is your last day
Because you never know just when your last day will be
As If It Is Your Last Day

Enough Time

God has given us enough time
Enough time to come to see, understand, and realize
That we desperately need Him in our lives
God has given us enough time
Enough time to search for true wisdom and knowledge
And true wisdom and knowledge to find
God has given us enough time
Enough time to diligently seek and find His face
Enough time to come to know of His mighty mercy
And of His awesome and wondrous saving grace
God has given us enough time
Enough time to come to know
Of His great agape love for all Mankind
God has given us enough time
Enough time to know that He is still omnipotent, all-powerful, and holy
Enough time to lift His name up high and give Him all the praise and glory
God has given us enough time
Enough time to come to lean, trust, and depend only upon Him
Enough time to surrender all and turn our lives completely over to Him
God has given us enough time
Enough time to realize that we cannot make it on our own
Enough time to turn from sin and come back home
God has given us enough time
Enough time to realize that we need one another
And that whether we like it or not
We're all true sisters and brothers
God has given us enough time
Enough time to learn our lessons and learn them well
Enough time to choose between Heaven or Hell
God has given us enough time
Enough Time

The Only Thing That Will Matter

The only thing that will matter in the end
Is how much we loved God and also our fellow man
It will not matter how much money we've got
Whether we acquired a little or if we acquired a lot
Because the only thing that will matter in the end
Is how much we loved God and also our fellow man
It will not matter how much knowledge we've learned
Or how many Master Degrees or PhD's we've earned
It will not matter what kind of cars we drove
Or the kind of neighborhood or community we lived in
Because the only thing that will matter in the end
Is how much we loved God and also our fellow man
It will not matter what kind of shoes or clothes we wore
Whether they were rags or the top of the line
It will not matter our age, shape, skin color, or our size
Whether we were underweight, overweight, or so-called fine
Because the only thing that will matter in the end
Is how much we loved God and also our fellow man
It will not matter how we appeared to our peers
It will only matter how we appear to the Lord
For, according to His judgment and His judgment alone
Will be our just, righteous, and eternal reward
Because the only thing that will matter in the end
Is how much we loved God and also our fellow man
The Only Thing That Will Matter

Come Inside   *Beverly Leonard*

Sooner or Later

Sooner or later, we're going to wake up and clearly see
That life is not a dream, a fairy tale, nor is it a fantasy
But we'll see that life is indeed a real and raw reality
Yes, soon or later, we're going to wake up and this we shall see

Sooner or later, we must learn and discern our lessons of life
Lessons learned through good times and times of sadness and strife
Yes, sooner or later, we must learn and discern our lessons of life

Sooner or later, what we sow in life we shall surely reap
Our fruit will either lift us up or knock us off our feet
Yes, sooner or later, what we sow in life we shall surely reap

Sooner or later, life will make us break down and cry
Sometimes we'll hurt so badly, it'll make us ask, "Oh, Lord, why"
Yes, sooner or later, life will make us break down and cry

Sooner or later, someone will try to steal our peace and joy
But if these very things are found in the realm of the Lord
These very things they'll be unable to take away or destroy
Yes, sooner or later, someone will try to steal our peace and joy

Sooner or later, someone will try to stab us in our backs
And the moment our backs are turned
Will be the moment they'll try to attack
Yes, sooner or later, someone will try to stab us in our backs

Sooner or later, someone will speak ill against me and you
Saying mean, malicious, and hurtful things that are just untrue
Yes, sooner or later, someone will speak ill against me and you

Sooner or later, someone will offer us something we don't need
And these kinds of people we'd better beware of and take heed
Yes, sooner or later, someone will offer us something we don't need

Sooner or later, someone we love will succumb to death and die
And please know, my beloved, that sin is the primary reason why
Yes, sooner or later, someone we love will succumb to death and die

Come Inside   *Beverly Leonard*

Sooner or later, if we keep on living, we're bound to get old
As our journey upon the Earth continues to unfurl and unfold
Yes, sooner or later, if we keep on living, we're bound to get old

Sooner or later, Jesus will return with the clouds
And every eye shall behold His glory and every knee shall surely bow
Yes, sooner or later, Jesus will return with the clouds

Sooner or later, we all shall stand before His holy throne
And He shall judge us according to how much love we have shown
Yes, sooner or later, we all shall stand before His holy throne
Sooner or Later

~ ~ ~

If You Get Anything Out of Life

If you get anything out of life
Get to know the love of God and of His beloved Son Jesus Christ
Yes, if you get anything out of life
Get to know first hand the love of God and Jesus Christ
If you get anything out of life
Get to know the joy that is found in God's holy realm
It's a joy the world can't give, nor can it take away or destroy
For, it's a joy that is found only in Him
Yes, if you get anything out of life
Get to know the joy found in God's holy realm
If you get anything out of life
Get true wisdom, knowledge, and discernment as well
For these very things, when used according to God's holy will
Will help prevent your soul from burning in the depths of Hell
Yes, if you get anything out of life
Get true wisdom, knowledge, and discernment as well
And make sure you get love and be sure to give love in return
For love shall cover a multitude of our sins in the very end
Yes, if you get anything out of life
Get love and be sure to give lots of love in return
It You Get Anything Out of Life

The Longer I Live

The longer I live the more clearly I can see
Just how much the Lord really cares for and loves me
Yes, the longer I live the more clearly this I can see

The longer I live the more I come to understand and know
That, to the Lord for any and everything, I can always freely go
Yes, the longer I live the more of the Lord's goodness I come to know

The longer I live the more I learn and discern my lessons of life
As I struggle through my trails, my tribulations, and my strife
Yes, the longer I live the more I learn and discern my lessons of life

The longer I live the more I learn to trust in the Lord
For, if I call upon Him, He'll be with me in both good times and hard
Yes, the longer I live the more I learn to trust in the Lord

The longer I live the more my faith grows each and every day
For, in times of trouble and woe, the Lord always makes a way
Yes, the longer I live the more my faith grows each and every day

The longer I live the more aches and pains I shall surely feel
More visits to the doctor's office and more prescription pills
Yes, the longer I live the more aches and pains I shall surely feel

The longer I live the more tears I will surely shed
Tears for the plight of the living and tears for the dead
Yes, the longer I live the more tears I will surely shed

The longer I live the closer I get to my journey's end
And if I endure, with the Lord in Paradise I shall forever spend
Yes, the longer I live the closer I get to my journey's end
The Longer I Live

Come Inside *Beverly Leonard*

Time Out

Time out for ignorance, impoliteness, and disrespect
Time out for disregard, carelessness, and neglect
Time out for ugly, mean, and negative attitudes
Time out for acting obnoxious, uncaring, and down-right rude
Time out for being abusive, offensive, violent, and cruel
Time out for acting like erratic, loony, and crazy fools
Time out for bigotry, bitterness, racism, and greed
Time out for sowing putrid, pungent, and negative seeds
Time out for injustice, disparity, and inequality
Time out for envy, resentment, hatred, scorn, and jealousy
Time out for broken, distressed, and shattered homes
Time out for families not loving one another and getting along
Time out for parents not parenting as they know they should
Time out for children who won't listen, obey, and be good
Time out for hard drinking and also hard drugging
Time out for gang-banging, sagging, and thugging
Time out for lying, cheating, coveting, and stealing
Time out for carnage, bloodshed, violence, and killing
Time out for crime, chaos, conflict, and corruption
Time out for wars, devastation, ruin, and destruction
Time out for the Races of Mankind not coming together as one
Time out for not putting God first and also His beloved Son
Time Out

~ ~ ~

In Spirit and In Truth

It doesn't matter where we worship the Lord
Just as long as we worship Him in spirit and in truth
In spirit, we connect our God-given spirit that is found inside us
To God's Holy Spirit that is holy, hallowed, and divine
A strong spiritual connection that is joined and aligned
And it is in truth with an honest and sincere heart
That we humbly enter into His heavenly and holy realm
And give all the honor, praise, and glory to Him
So, you see, it doesn't matter where we worship the Lord
Just as long as we worship Him in spirit and in truth
In Spirit and In Truth

Before the Setting of the Sun

If I should die this very day before the setting of the sun
What final farewells would I leave behind
What last words would I express to everyone
I would first have to free my mind and also my heart
From any negative feelings and emotions felt
I would have to loose and let go of the pains of the past
And of any hard feelings and grudges kept

I would then gather my loved ones all around
And build bridges if there were none to cross
I would tell them of my undying love and devotion for them
Before the last moments of my life are over and lost
I would tell them to be strong and to hold on together
And to seek the comfort that is found only in the good Lord
For He is the one who is able to carry us through
When times get difficult, stressful, painful, and rock-hard
I would tell my beloved children to continue to be good
And to always do the things that they know they should
Yes, I would express my love for my loved ones
Before the setting of the sun

To my beloved mate I would say farewell and good-bye
And thank him for all of the times that together we had
For together we trudged through thick and through thin
Through both the happy times and also the sad
Yes, I would say farewell to my beloved mate
And remind him to keep an ever-watchful eye on our little ones
Before the setting of the sun

To my loving parents I would say a heart-felt thank you
For loving and nurturing me in an unconditional way
For without their guidance and their undying love for me
Where, pray tell, would I be in the world today
Yes, I would thank my loving parents for a job well done
Before the setting of the sun

Come Inside   *Beverly Leonard*

To my sisters and my brothers
Blood of my blood and genes of my genes
I would say let not my death be in vain
But let it be a time to heal old wounds and end old pains
And to waste not another moment on sorrows and regrets from the past
Or heartaches and sorrows are sure to last and last
Yes, I would tell my sisters and my brothers
Let us come together as one
Before the setting of the sun

To my dear friends who were always there for me
Through the good times as well as through the bad
Thank you for the laughter, the jokes, and the tears that we shared
Thank you for all the good times that together we had
Yes, I would thank my dear friends who were always there for me
Before the setting of the sun

To all the children of the world
To God's precious little boys and girls
I would remind them of the great love that God has for them
And of the blessings that are found only in Him and in His holy realm
I would tell them to do their part to help spread joy and peace
And to remember that they are the heirs of glorious things to come
If they remember where and from whom they come from
I would remind them that their Heavenly Father loves them so
And that to Him for any and everything they can always freely go
Yes, I would remind the children of the great love God has for them
Before the setting of the sun

To the young men and women of the world
I would say be strong and continue to press on
And though sometimes the goings may get a little bit rough
Remember that God is still sitting on His mighty throne
And if you call upon His name, He'll strengthen and fortify you
He will lift you up and help you make it through
So, have faith in Him and always follow His righteous lead
Be watchful and ever so mindful of life's many pitfalls and traps
Believe in yourselves and you will prosper, excel, and succeed
Yes, I would tell the young men and women these very things
Before the setting of the sun

Come Inside   *Beverly Leonard*

To the parents of the world
Love your children, train your children, and teach them well
Teach them through your fine examples and they will excel
And remember, parents, there is a Heaven and there is a Hell
Yes, I would stress to the parents the importance of parenting
Before the setting of the sun

To my Black brothers and sisters
The true salt of all the Earth
I would say, for too long we have depended on others to lead us
But now it is time for our glorious and long over-due rebirth
It is time to rise, my beautiful Black people
And come together as One before the setting of the sun
For this is the only way that the salvation of our people can be done

To ALL my brothers and sisters around the world
For, from the original pair, we all came to be
Moreover, we all came from the Creator who created the Earth
To be home for the entire Human family
But because of greed and the tendency to dominate one another
We have not lived according to His Word as sisters and brothers
But the Lord is coming soon to set matter straight
So, let us come together now before it is too late
Let us come together as one before the setting of the sun

To those who judge others by the color of their skin
Please know that you will surely meet your Maker one day
And the Lord will not be happy, proud, or pleased
With your bigot, evil, ugly, hurtful, and hateful ways
You'd better clean your heart out now and fill it with love
Do it now before the setting of the sun

And now, as the sun begins to set upon the horizon
And upon my life for the very last time
A sense of peace and tranquility shall overcome me
For by then I shall have freed my heart and also my mind
Yes, peace and tranquility shall overcome me
Before the setting of the sun

Come Inside *Beverly Leonard*

And into a quiet place I shall retreat
Into the sanctuary of my mind
And I'll ask the Lord to receive my spirit
After I exhale for the very last time
But before I breathe my very last breath
I shall pray for those that I leave behind
I shall ask the Lord to please guide, bless, and protect them
And that true joy and happiness they shall one day find

Now as my eyes begin to dim upon this earthly realm
They shall come into focus with a spiritual view
For I shall behold the heavenly hosts of angels
For they shall come to comfort and guide me safely through
Yes, the angels will come to comfort and guide me
Before the setting of the sun

My last message to the world would be of love
For, love is the key, it always was, and it always will be
Now, I bid you farewell, adieu, and good-bye
For the sun has now set in the late evening sky
~
If today was your last day before the setting of the sun
What final farewells would you express to everyone
Before the Setting of the Sun

Things Remembered

A man can do many good things in life
But, all too often, he will be remembered
For the single flaw or fault that was done
And all the good that he did will be forgotten or pushed to the side
Such a pity, but such is the way of the human mind
Yes, a man can do a multitude of good deeds and only one bad sin
And be cast into the dark depths of the mind by mortal men
But I'm so glad that God is most merciful, gracious, forgiving, and kind
For, it is not the single flaw, but the multitude of good
That will come to the Lord's mind on Judgment Day
And all the good that we have done
Will cover and wash our sins away
Things Remembered

~ ~ ~

Something New

When one chapter ends, a new chapter begins
When earthly death overcomes earthly life
Into a spiritual realm we enter and ascend
And the end of the road leads to yet another
So, to all my earthly sisters and brothers
I pray that you have taken these messages to heart
Messages sent down from Heaven above
Messages of hope, good will, compassion, peace, and love
And by the divine grace and mercy of the good Lord
Unto me new messages may He continue to send
Messages from on high to deliver to earthly men
For the end is not the end, but it is the beginning
The beginning of something new
Something New

When It All Boils Down To It

When it all boils down to it
It will not matter *what* perils we went through in life
But what will matter the most
Is *how* we went through our trials, our tribulations, and strife
Whether we tripped and stumbled and cursed the good Lord
Or whether we kept our integrity in both good times and hard

Now, you may recall the story of Job who suffered like no other
He lost his friends, his wealth, his fortune, and also his good health
He lost his children who were very precious and dear to his heart
But through it all, Job kept his integrity
And from the Word of the Lord, Job did not depart

Yes, when it all boils down to it
It will not matter *what* perils we went through in life
For life is full of tribulations, temptations, hardships, and strife
We will all go through some things, this there is no doubt
But we must be very careful as to *how* we go through them
For *how* we deal with life's dilemmas
Will greatly affect how our future will turn out

So, when hard times come like they always do
We must cling to our faith and our integrity, too
We must call upon the good Lord in both good times and hard
For He has the power to deliver us and see us safely through

Yes, when it all boils down to it
It's not *what* we go through in life
But it's *how* we go through it
When It All Boils Down To It

Let Your Light Shine

Like dewdrops on the morning grass
Our lives can sometimes be
For one day we're here and the next day we're gone
Only to become a faint and distant memory
So much precious time we squander and waste
On things that are small, insignificant, trivial, and trite
Realizing not that the candle burns on
And soon the darkness overshadows the light
So, while our light continues to shine
We must use it to help one another
To lift, to love, to guide, to inspire
And to encourage our sisters and our brothers
So that when our light ceases to shine
And a new day is about to dawn
Our love for life, living, and for one another
Shall continue to live on
Yes, our lives will live on through the lives of others
Whom we have helped and befriended along life's way
And with hope and faith within our hearts
We'll all be reunited with them again some day
Let Your Light Shine

~ ~ ~

Do Your Part

No one can do everything, but everyone can do something
To help make this world a better place in which to live
So, as you live your life from day to day
Make sure that you do your part and give
And just think, if I do my part and you do your part
And he does his part and she does her part, too
There would be no parts left undone to do
So, do your part, and may God continue to bless you
Do Your Part

Be

Be loving and honest
Be kind and fair
Be caring and courteous
Be nice and polite
Be joyful and rejoice
Be thoughtful and considerate
Be sympathetic and compassionate
Be respectful and well-mannered
Be alert and conscious
Be cautious and careful
Be gracious and merciful
Be understanding and forgiving
Be patient and prayerful
Be productive and industrious
Be calm and self-controlled
Be faithful and loyal
Be dedicated and sincere
Be trustworthy and true
Be diligent and determined
Be reliable and dependable
Be perceptive and observant
Be sensible and wise
Be fast to listen and slow to speak
Be persistent when need be
Be hopeful, humble, and happy
Be all that you can be
Be helpful and supportive
Be reasonable and responsible
Be genuine and real
Be encouraged and of good cheer
Be blessed and thankful
Be zealous and steadfast
Be strong, hold on, and endure
Be not afraid, but fear the Lord
Be assured that God loves you
Be ready when Jesus comes
Be

Task Completed

If the words that are found within
Touched someone in any kind of way
Whether they moved someone, inspired someone
Caused someone to have a better and brighter day
Taught someone something or guided someone along the way
Whether they motivated someone or enlightened someone
Brought comfort to someone or caused someone to kneel down and to pray
Whether they encouraged someone on the narrow path to stay
Brought someone to the Lord or turned someone around
Caused someone to smile or lifted someone to higher ground
If the words that are found within
Touched someone in any kind of way
Then my task is completed
Task Completed

~ ~ ~

Goodnight

My eyes are tired and my fingers hurt
I'm physically drained though still mentally alert
And though my mind is still going strong
My body is weak and it can't continue on
So, I'll put down my paper and also my pen
And say goodnight to earthly men
I bid you sweet dreams and a sweet adieu
Until the next time I take a walk with you
Good Night

Come Inside　　　　　　　　　　　　　*Beverly Leonard*

A Special Tribute to Marvin Pentz Gaye, Jr.

The Man, His Message, and His Music

Come Inside *Beverly Leonard*

A Special Tribute to Marvin Pentz Gaye, Jr.

The Man, His Message, and His Music
April 2, 1939 - April 1, 1984

~ Marvin ~

What words can I choose to capture your spirit
For, your spirit is like the untamed winds that gust and blow
Soaring high like an eagle to lofty mountaintops
Then plunging and plummeting into valleys down below

Bounding, running, leaping, and then falling
Then standing and starting all over again
Sometimes quiet, sullen, moody, and restless
Other times intense, fleeting, brisk, and breathless

A continuous movement of energy in motion
Always on the move, yet, never reaching a final destination
Unrestricted, unhindered, and unrestrained
Two powerful and forceful masterpieces of creation

Marvin, your spirit runs free like liquid love
Unable to be captured, caught, or contained
And though physically you are away from us
Spiritually, with us, you will always remain

~

The Lord needed an angel to deliver His holy message
To the masses of Mankind who lived upon the Earth
So, He looked around and many willing servants He found
But He needed someone extra-special for this special rebirth

He then looked upon His heavenly choir
Especially upon the one who sang out so beautifully
And when asked to deliver God's message of love to Mankind
This heavenly host quickly answered, "Yes, Lord, please send me"

Come Inside
Beverly Leonard

It was a sad, yet, joyous occasion
When the Lord released this heavenly spirit from Heaven above
For all would surely miss his presence up in Heaven
But they all knew he had to go forth with God's message of love

~

It was a Sunday morning in Washington, D. C.
When a man-child babe was born into a Black family
Born the son of a gentle woman and a preacher man
This child was destined to spread love all across the land

In a Pentecostal home Marvin was reared and raised
And the Lord's holy name he lifted and praised
With a natural ear for music, he sang with great passion and joy
But deep, deep inside lived a terrified and tortured little boy

For, even though his father preached of God's undying love
His father failed to show true love and affection toward his son
And this would affect Marvin all the days of his life
Filling him with insecurities, confusion, mental chaos, and strife

But Marvin found comfort and solace in his music
For, it was an outlet in which he purged his anxieties and fears
Inspired by such great ones as Marian, Mahalia, and Lady Day
Marvin sang out to chase his blues away

The sensuous movements of his swaying hips
And the words of love which poured from his lips
Stirred the hearts of both the young and the old
For, Marvin was a musical genius - gifted, talented, and bold

Together, Marvin and Tammi sang of love, happiness, and romance
To rhythms that made everyone finger-pop, toe-tap, and dance
But heartache soon came, for Tammi's young life, death did claim
And singing with another was never, for Marvin, quite the same

Come Inside *Beverly Leonard*

It seemed as if the world was crashing in all around him
Violence and racism were running rampant all across the land
Marvin knew that he had to make a positive impact on Mankind
Yes, Marvin knew in his heart that it was time to take a stand

Soon his songs of romance became songs of the realities of life
For, with sensitive insight, Marvin saw what was really going on
And it pained his heart to see the world so divided and torn apart
So, he spoke out through the words of his powerful songs

Save the babies, he told the world
And save our beautiful planet, too
For, how much more can our world endure
Marvin said there was only one real and perfect cure

He sang of God's goodness, His mercy, and of His love
For Marvin was now realizing his true calling from above
He claimed and maintained that all God ever asked of Mankind
Was that we give each other love and true love we would find

But Marvin was a troubled young man
Sometimes he was a stubborn kind of guy
He became hooked, my friends, on artificial happiness
Which sent him reeling and flying into the friendly sky

It was a constant battle that ranted, roared, and raged
Within the depths and darkness of Marvin's tormented mind
And even though he sang of true love, peace, and happiness
These very things eluded Marvin's life nearly every time

He felt that the end of his road was near
For, he was now consumed by a sick and paranoid fear
It seemed, for Marvin, to be just one heartache after another
As if his spirit was ready to leave this world and move on to another

Then all too soon, but right on time
The angels of death came to receive him
For, the Lord saw his hurt and He knew his pain
The Lord knew that Marvin's life had become dark and dim

So, the Lord released him from his cares and from his fears
He said, "Marvin, no more heartaches and no more tears
Return to me and to my unchanging love
Return to your original position in Heaven above"

~

It was a Sunday morning when Marvin went away
The terrible tragedy happened on April Fool's Day
But it wasn't a joke, for it saddened the Earth
But sad as it was, it was time for Marvin's heavenly rebirth

Now his spirit is free and again with the angels he sings
Songs of pure love that only pure love can bring
And I pray that one day his sweet voice again I'll hear
His soulful and stirring melodies upon my awaiting ear

But until then, I'll treasure the music that Marvin left behind
And the messages they still seek to bring
And may they continue to soar over space and time
Soaring far and wide on an eagle's wing

Thank you, Marvin, for your messages and for your music
And thank you, Heavenly Father, for the life of this gentle man
Now, I bid you a sweet adieu, Marvin
Until I see your sweet face once again

Peace and Love

**Coming soon
"Enter At Your Own Risk"**

www.ingramcontent.com/pod-product-compliance
Lightning Source LLC
Chambersburg PA
CBHW022054160426
43198CB00008B/222